Sri Sukta

Tantra of Inner Prosperity

ALSO BY PANDIT RAJMANI TIGUNAIT, PHD

BOOKS

Vishoka Meditation: The Yoga of Inner Radiance

The Practice of the Yoga Sutra: Sadhana Pada

The Secret of the Yoga Sutra: Samadhi Pada

The Pursuit of Power and Freedom: Katha Upanishad

Touched by Fire: The Ongoing Journey of a Spiritual Seeker

Lighting the Flame of Compassion

Inner Quest: Yoga's Answers to Life's Questions

The Himalayan Masters: A Living Tradition

Why We Fight: Practices for Lasting Peace

At the Eleventh Hour: The Biography of Swami Rama

Swami Rama of the Himalayas: His Life and Mission

Tantra Unveiled: Seducing the Forces of Matter and Spirit

Shakti: The Power in Tantra (A Scholarly Approach)

From Death to Birth: Understanding Karma and Reincarnation

The Power of Mantra and the Mystery of Initiation

Shakti Sadhana: Steps to Samadhi

Seven Systems of Indian Philosophy

AUDIO & VIDEO

Living Tantra Series DVD set

Spirit of the Vedas

Spirit of the Upanishads

Pulsation: Chants of the Maha Kumbha Mela

Sri Sukta

Tantra of Inner Prosperity

PANDIT RAJMANI TIGUNAIT, PhD

HIMALAYAN INSTITUTE®

HONESDALE, PENNSYLVANIA USA

Himalayan Institute
952 Bethany Turnpike
Honesdale, PA 18431

HimalayanInstitute.org

Printed in the United States of America

23 22 21 20 1 2 3 4 5

ISBN-13: 978-0-89389-291-3 (paper)

Cover art by Meera Tigunait

Library of Congress Control Number: 2020905585

∞ This paper meets the requirements of ANSI/NISO Z39-48-1992 (Permanence of Paper).

Contents

Preface vii

Introduction 1

The Power and Mystery of Sri Sukta 9

Deeper Understanding of Poverty and Prosperity 10

Constant Awareness of Omniscient Reality 18

A Personal Bond with the Seers of Sri Sukta 22

The Exposition of Sri Sukta 27

Mantras 1–16

The Practice of Sri Sukta 91

Starting Out 93

Formal Practice: Stage One 96

Formal Practice: Stage Two 98

Formal Practice: Stage Three 105

Appendices

A: Sri Sukta Mantras 115

B: The Sri Vidya Tradition 133

Preface

I was born into a family of pandits. Our wealth and social status were measured by our knowledge of ancient scriptures and our commitment to spiritual practices. I do not remember what toys I had as a child or what kind of games I played, but I do remember how proud and joyful my parents were when I memorized Sri Sukta.

When my Sanskrit teachers came to know how sincerely I recited Sri Sukta every day, they began to teach texts and subjects that had nothing to do with our formal coursework. They introduced me to the scripture *Durga Saptashati* and taught me how Sri Sukta fulfills all the criteria for undertaking the higher practices of tantra yoga.

Eventually, my most senior Sanskrit teacher initiated me into the *navarna* mantra. Thereafter, the floodgate of Vedic and tantric studies opened. Later, two great souls, Swami Sadananda and Swami Rama, took my study and practice to a place of which my tongue cannot speak.

This current work is an effort to express my gratitude to Divine Providence, who in her own mysterious way uses me as a conduit to descend into the minds and hearts of all those who study and practice Sri Sukta.

SRI SUKTA

Introduction

Sri Sukta is part of the *Rig Veda*, the most ancient of the world's sacred scriptures. Many centuries ago, the great sage Vyasa organized the thousands of mantras of the *Rig Veda* into clusters. The technical name for these clusters is *sukta*. Each sukta has a unique mantric power, function, and purpose. The concluding clusters of mantras in the *Rig Veda* are known as Khila Suktas or Khailakani Suktani. *Khila* means "the space that gives room to a newly emerging reality." It is a clutter-free, unobstructed power that attracts the forces of fullness and abundance and displaces the conditions of emptiness, loneliness, purposelessness, and worthlessness.

The Khila Suktas address the concerns of daily life. The seers of these mantras acknowledge that achieving ultimate freedom and lasting fulfillment is the highest goal of life, and are adamant that we can achieve this lofty goal only if our body is strong and our mind is clear. Safety in the external world is necessary if we are to seek and find safety in the inner world. Inner prosperity is a far-fetched dream if the majority of our time and energy is consumed in meeting our daily needs. The Khila Suktas are dedicated to securing safety, security, and prosperity at the mundane level, and to guiding us to use these gifts as a gateway to inner safety, security, and prosperity. In addition, these suktas guide us to use the forces of inner protection and prosperity to further enrich our life in the external world. Once the wheels of inner and outer safety, security, and protection are in motion, living on this mortal plane is a joy. The idea of finding freedom in heaven loses its luster for we have found it right here in this world.

Sri Sukta is one of the Khila Suktas. It consists of sixteen mantras. The first fifteen mantras invoke the sacred fire and request it to bring the presiding forces of health, wealth, peace, and prosperity to us. The sixteenth mantra proclaims that the recitation of the first fifteen mantras awakens the infallible power of the divine force that rules over the conditions resulting in inner and outer prosperity.

The practice of Sri Sukta is grounded in a philosophy that sees this world as a manifestation of divine will. This philosophy is an extension of a much larger body of wisdom and experience known as Sri Vidya. A perfect blend of the Vedic and tantric traditions, Sri Vidya espouses a nondualistic philosophy. According to this philosophy, there is only one reality. Absolute, nameless, and formless, it is the locus for everything that exists. Yogis of the highest caliber experience this reality as waves of joy and beauty—*ananda lahari* and *saundarya lahari*. This experience awakens the inherent power of intuition, enabling a yogi to see the entire phenomenal world as a wave of joy and beauty.

Sitting at the peak of this experience, the great sage Dakshinamurti saw the undivided truth pertaining to both unmanifest and manifest reality. He saw that every aspect of manifest reality—the phenomenal world—contains the same joy and beauty inherent in unmanifest, transcendental reality. He also saw that although most of that joy and beauty remains dormant in the phenomenal world, human beings have the power to awaken it—a power that depends heavily on how awakened they are themselves. Meditation is the surest way to that inner awakening. The soul of meditation is the power of mantra. The spiritual practice based on the experience of the sage Dakshinamurti came to be known as Sri Vidya. Sri Sukta is one of the cardinal texts leading to the experience of Sri Vidya.

The advanced practices of Sri Sukta are closely guarded by the living tradition. However, casual practices are widespread across all Indian traditions and subtraditions. According to popular belief, Sri Sukta is a prayer to Lakshmi, the goddess of wealth, a belief that incentivizes the masses to practice Sri Sukta casually. For example, people often recite it with the intention of overcoming a financial problem. Only highly motivated seekers attempt to unravel its potent content and profound intent.

The Sri Vidya tradition prescribes the practice of Sri Sukta to calm inner storms and the destruction caused by them. Almost without exception, all of us are caught in storms of doubt, fear, worry, anger, hatred, greed, resentment, regret, and feelings of helplessness, unworthiness, and despondency. These storms damage our trust in ourselves, in our loved ones, in justice, and in divine providence. We become weak and impoverished from inside. Our inner weakness and poverty affect our family and our surroundings. Inner poverty blocks our ability to see the abundant gifts inherent in nature and in our relationships with others. The ultimate goal of Sri Sukta practice is to eliminate our inner poverty and empower us to experience the fullness of life.

The practice of Sri Sukta is done in three successive stages. The first stage helps us to cultivate a feeling for the mantras and their seers and to discover our relationship with them. It also helps us transform our intellectual understanding of these mantras into a living experience. This stage of the practice enables us to internalize the mantras, demolishing the conceptual wall of duality that separates earth from heaven and humans from divine beings. The mantras become part of our consciousness, and we become part of the mantric field. This merger sheds new light on our spiritual quest. We no longer see ourselves as pitiful and impoverished, begging an outside source for rescue. Rather, we do the practice joyfully to further strengthen our bond with the divinity within. Our practice is empowered by the understanding that the forces of abundance have always been with us, and that the recitation of mantras is a way to experience their presence at a conscious level.

As this understanding matures, we find ourselves drawn to the practice spontaneously and effortlessly. We do our practice not in response to worldly pressures but because there is no better way to express our gratitude to the benevolent forces of nature who have been constantly showering us with everything we need. The pathetic and needy being in us has vanished. This is how this first stage prepares the enthusiastic, joyful, and trusting being in us to undertake the next level of the practice.

The second stage is more intense than the first stage. The core of the practice consists of reciting the entire Sri Sukta eight hundred times in eleven days. Unlike the first stage, where rules and regulations pertaining to the practice are somewhat relaxed, in the second stage strict rules govern when to start and conclude the practice. Both the time and the place to undertake this practice are highly regulated. Furthermore, the number of recitations done on each day is precisely fixed and must be strictly observed. The fire offering is an integral part of the practice at this stage. Mental disciplines; mastery over inner tendencies; and special observances regarding thought, speech, and action are of paramount importance.

The goal is to reach a state of mantric absorption profound enough to create deep grooves in our consciousness. This causes the highly compressed mantric shakti of Sri Sukta to outshine previously stored negative tendencies, rendering them inert. This stage of practice creates space in our consciousness fit to be occupied by the seers of the mantras. This allows us to see the mantras through the eyes of the seers. Although intellectually we may not comprehend the full scope of mantra shakti, at the spiritual level we are bathing in it.

If we complete the second stage of practice with perfection and precision, we are able to transmit the mantras of Sri Sukta to other seekers, just as nature's forces—the sun, water, fire, and air—transmit nourishment to all living beings. In other words, we become a conduit for transmitting the gifts of love, wisdom, compassion, protection, and nourishment inherent in Sri Sukta. This privilege allows us to take the practice to the next level.

The third and final stage of the practice is a highly guarded secret of the tradition. It is never done for personal benefit, but only for the benefit of humanity. More precisely, it is done in service of Mother Nature, who is the repository of true protection, nourishment, and prosperity. Maha Pushti Yaga is an example of this third stage of practice.

Maha Pushti Yaga means "group practice of great nourishment." The goal of this practice is to awaken the benevolent forces of nature that provide nourishment to all living beings. The main focus of this practice is the nullification of fourteen conditions that drain the sap of life and the creation of the conditions for eighteen categories of peace to manifest. The fourteen conditions that drain the sap of life include emptiness, loneliness, and purposelessness; grief and feelings of regret; and the tendency to harm oneself and others. The eighteen categories of peace include an overarching atmosphere of stability, security, and protection; an atmosphere free of anger, fear, and violence; and an atmosphere free of poverty and disease.

The practice of Maha Pushti Yaga is both powerful and rare. It is highly technical and requires that the officiating yogi be well versed in the advanced tantric practices of Rudra Yaga, Sri Chakra sadhana, and most importantly, the secret science and practice of Jatavedas Agni. The preparatory and ancillary practices associated with this stage of Sri Sukta sadhana are as important as in the main body of the practice; the observances at this stage are even stricter than those in the second stage. A precise description of the third stage of Sri Sukta is beyond the scope of this present volume.

This volume has a twofold purpose: to expound the meaning of the Sri Sukta mantras and to delineate the practices that constitute the first two stages of Sri Sukta sadhana. While expounding this text, my biggest challenge has been to transport the intended meaning of the mantras from Sanskrit to English without distorting or contaminating their mantric spirit. Sri Sukta was revealed in its current form long before the seventh century BCE, when the great grammarian Panini gave a formal structure to Sanskrit, known today as classical Sanskrit. Sri Sukta is not in classical Sanskrit but in Vedic Sanskrit. Therefore, following in the footsteps of ancient commentators, I have used the *nirukti* methodology of expounding the meaning of words, which predates the grammatical rules outlined by Panini. The other challenge I faced was translating words that have a double or triple meaning, a significant mythological meaning, or a specialized meaning in different fields of knowledge. In expounding such words and concepts, I have taken the liberty of siding with the precepts of the Sri Vidya tradition; in doing so, I have also tried my best to respect academic sensitivities.

In regard to delineating Sri Sukta sadhana in three successive stages, I have relied on two main sources: how I was led to practice it, and how the great master Vidyaranya Yati describes it in his monumental work *Sri Vidyarnava.* As a boy, I recited Sri Sukta as a prayer to the Divine Mother. Later, I was guided to recite it as an ancillary practice to the recitation of another scripture, *Durga Saptashati.* Still later, I was guided to recite Sri Sukta as part of my sadhana of the *navarna* mantra, the nine-syllable mantra of the Divine Mother in the form of Durga. In between, my teachers introduced the *gayatri* mantra and the *maha mrityunjaya* mantra. When I read the voluminous text *Sri Vidyarnava,* which elaborates the practice of Sri Sukta along with a long list of injunctions, I came to realize why my teachers in earlier days helped me take baby steps.

Using my common sense, as well as guidance from the scriptures and the living tradition, I have delineated the entire course of Sri Sukta sadhana in this volume. Although it is nowhere close to being an exhaustive exposition of Sri Sukta, this volume is a good start. I am grateful to the sages of the tradition and to the divinities who use Sri Sukta as their locus for choosing me as an instrument for bringing this text to seekers of happiness and inner prosperity.

The Power and Mystery of Sri Sukta

From the standpoint of practice, Sri Sukta is one of the cardinal texts of tantra, particularly of the Sri Vidya tradition. It consists of fifteen mantras, each an unimaginably vast pool of power and wisdom. What distinguishes this scripture from thousands of others is its affirmation that there is an abundance of joy and beauty in the world, and that living in this world is a blessing. Prosperity, both inner and outer, is intrinsic to nature's DNA and everything that issues from it. Poverty and decrepitude indicate we are disconnected from nature's abundance. Internal and external poverty, feelings of emptiness and loneliness, and lack of self-worth are not part of nature's design—they are our own creation. Demolishing our self-created misery, reclaiming the joy of abundance inherent in every aspect of life, and inviting that joy to fill our inner and outer worlds is the message of Sri Sukta.

In popular tantric circles these mantras are used to combat poverty, disease, and family disharmony, and to overcome the causes of recurring failure. In these circles, adepts prescribe the entire Sri Sukta, or one particular mantra, to achieve specific goals. For example, in order to overcome cyclical failure and bring stability in business ventures, they prescribe the second mantra. To help a seeker secure a position marked by power, prestige, and glamour, they prescribe the third mantra. For healing, rapid recovery, and nourishment, they design a practice with the ninth mantra at its core.

In the inner circle of the Sri Vidya tradition, however, the practice of Sri Sukta is undertaken to create a new reality, one that cannot be subdued by the forces of darkness. Sri Sukta is a practice for inner awakening and unfoldment. The ultimate goal of practicing Sri Sukta is to find our connection with the divinity that resides in all of us, and which manifests in the space of our consciousness as a wave of beauty and joy. It is about finding and eventually embodying the richness of our mind and soul, and infusing every breath with that richness. It is about living a healthy, happy, peaceful, and prosperous life.

When expounding on the power and mystery of Sri Sukta, adepts compare it with a safe-deposit box. Sri Sukta is firmly anchored in a secure space—the space of pure revelation—surrounded by the impenetrable wall of *prakriti,* primordial nature. In order to walk through this impenetrable wall, enter the field of pure revelation, open the safe, and claim ownership of the wealth it contains, we need three keys: a clear and accurate understanding of poverty and prosperity, a constant awareness of all-knowing omniscient reality, and a personal bond with the seer (*rishi*) who received the revelation of Sri Sukta.

Deeper Understanding of Poverty and Prosperity

Poverty is generally defined as the lack of sufficient means to meet daily needs, while prosperity means having bountiful resources to materialize desires, passions, and ambitions. According to the tradition of Sri Vidya, these definitions are simplistic and fail to convey the true meaning of the terms.

For the masters who received the revelation of Sri Sukta, the domain of poverty encompasses much more than lack of sufficient food, clothing, and shelter. Poverty is defined by deficiency. A person with little or no food, clothing, and shelter is clearly poor, but to an enlightened mind, so is a person with a weak body and mind. A person suffering from deficiency in minerals and enzymes is poor, as is a person with a compromised immune system. A person whose lungs, heart, liver, kidneys, nervous or endocrine systems are not functioning efficiently is poor. A person living in a household bereft of love and understanding is poor. A person suffering from loneliness and a sense of unworthiness is poor, as is a person lacking self-understanding, enthusiasm, courage, ambition, and confidence. Anyone deficient in creativity or the skill to put their knowledge into action is poor, as is anyone who is impressionable, dependent on the opinions of others, and lacking in determination. A person who gravitates toward low-grade thoughts and ideas, who engages in foul or destructive conversations, and who engages in mindless actions is poor.

The masters of Sri Vidya have observed that our inability to eat, digest, and assimilate food properly is a more severe form of poverty than lacking sufficient food. Our deeply ingrained habit of misusing and abusing resources has consequences far more severe than our inability to access plentiful resources. People deficient in the power of discernment are easily swept up in mass hysteria and, in the process, destabilize their lives, their families, and their societies. A wise person knows that suffering walks into our life more forcefully through such unidentified forms of poverty than through the more commonly identified forms. Anger, hatred, greed, fear, and attachment destroy our peace of mind. A fearful, restless mind robs us of our sleep. That is poverty. We are suffering from poverty when we become suspicious of our loved ones and concerned with protecting our assets from them.

In a socioeconomic context, we recognize communities without running water and electricity and with no access to education and health care as poor. But we are not accustomed to associating environmental degradation with poverty. We share a group poverty when we do not have clean air to breathe, clean water to drink, nutritious food to eat, or a quiet place to live. Because we consider drought, flood, wildfires, hurricanes, and tornados as natural, it rarely occurs to us that such events are due to an imbalance in nature, and at a subtle level, that this imbalance is due to our deficient relationship with the natural world. Similarly, we are embroiled in group poverty when we live in a society or nation rife with social injustice or ethnic or religious conflict—when men or women of various ethnic or religious groups are denied equal opportunities. These deficiencies are potent and far-reaching forms of poverty.

The fifteen mantras of Sri Sukta hold the key to driving away the entire range of poverty by embracing Lakshmi, the goddess of abundance, in the most fulfilling way. To the adepts of Sri Sukta, Lakshmi is not a female divinity who lives in heaven and is reachable solely by the blessed ones. She is with us, in us, and all around us. She is beyond number and gender. She is all pervasive. Time, space, and the law of cause and effect are her creation. She is as integral to us as our own self-awareness. She is the might of the almighty in us. She is as accessible to us as parents to their children and nutrients to every cell of our body. She is the vitality of our body, the pulsation of our breath, the brilliance of our mind, and the joy of our soul. According to Sri Sukta, the absence of this realization is the ground for all forms of poverty, both internal and external. Gaining this realization and becoming firm in it opens the floodgate of abundance inherent in us and in the natural world.

The manifestation of the goddess of abundance can be compared with a carving. There are numberless images contained in a piece of wood. Which image will emerge depends on the imagination and skill of the artist. Similarly, Lakshmi, the goddess of abundance, is intrinsically endowed with limitless attributes. Which attributes will emerge from her, with what intensity, and to what effect, depends on the unique quality of the shakti we use to invoke her. When we invoke her through Sri Sukta, she emerges and fills our inner and outer worlds with a prosperity unique to the quality of those fifteen mantras. When practiced with precision and the requisite preparations and precautions, these mantras emit powers that influence everything, from the subtlest aspects of reality to the most mundane. For the sake of simplicity and ease of comprehension, these powers and their effect on us are described in thirty categories.

The first is *Hiranyavarna*, the resplendent pulsation of the divine manifesting as the life force. It fills us with the conviction that we are descendants of a radiant being. Reclaiming our inner radiance is our birthright. Falling prey to darkness—denigrating thoughts, feelings, and behaviors—is to dishonor the ever-radiant being that accompanies us from breath to breath, and from birth to birth. As we will see, this theme is reinforced throughout Sri Sukta (SS 1).

The goddess invoked through Sri Sukta is garlanded with gold and silver. This is an indication of her superior taste. Her presence attenuates and eventually nullifies the negative tendencies that force us into low-grade actions (SS 1).

The practice of Sri Sukta awakens the shakti that brings stability to our life. This stability is characterized by the removal of cyclical failure. It makes our endeavors, as well as their results, sustainable (SS 2).

The energy of Sri Sukta creates an environment in which we must gain the recognition we deserve. We are accompanied by the shakti that prevents the crafty and greedy among us from claiming credit for our hard work (SS 3).

In the presence of the goddess of abundance as invoked by Sri Sukta, we are happy with others and others are happy with us. This removes all room for discord and conflict within us, our family, our community, and the society at large (SS 4).

Prosperity entering through the corridors of Sri Sukta makes us generous. We find joy in sharing the best of ourselves. We experience everyone and everything as an extension of the all-pervading divine force. Sharing the fruits of our endeavors with others becomes a way of worshipping the pervasive presence of the divine. The joy of giving overshadows the pain caused by lack of reciprocity (SS 5).

The company of the goddess emerging from the cloud of Sri Sukta makes us aware that the tree of our life has been planted by higher reality. It knows the intrinsic quality of that tree and the soil in which it is planted. It also knows the quality of the fruit this tree will bear. The job of the tree is to respond to nature's forces, which empower it to grow and bear fruit. This realization makes us work hard, while maintaining constant awareness of the reality that gives us the insight and strength to work hard. The constant awareness of higher reality fills us with enthusiasm and the courage to succeed, while remaining free from fear and anxiety (SS 6). We strive for prosperity, recognition, and prominence. We do everything in our power to excel, with full awareness that the fulfillment we derive from our achievements is an expression of her pleasure. This enables us to enjoy the fullness of life without attempting to possess it (SS 7).

Prosperity resulting from the practice of Sri Sukta is marked by freedom from five conditions that drain the sap of life from our inner and outer worlds: hunger, thirst, impurities, old age, and the feeling of emptiness. In the presence of the goddess of abundance emerging from the mantric field of Sri Sukta, we not only attain freedom from these five debilitating conditions, we also become acutely aware of the circumstances that create them. We know overcoming the biological causes of hunger and thirst is easier than overcoming the hunger for power and position and the insatiable thirst for sensory pleasure. The energy emitted by Sri Sukta creates an environment in which the hunger for power and the thirst for pleasure are supplanted by feelings of pride in sharing and a deep sense of contentment. We lose the taste for afflicting thought, speech, and action. Biological aging may proceed as scheduled but has no effect on the freshness of our mind. In her presence, the sense of emptiness evaporates. We become an integral part of a prosperity that cannot be measured (SS 8).

Prosperity emerging from the mantric shakti of Sri Sukta is further marked by four qualities: inner fragrance, unsuppressibility, lasting nurturance, and the ability to digest and assimilate. Inner fragrance refers to our very essence—the qualities of selfless love, compassion, and the impulse to work for the higher good. The prosperity invoked by Sri Sukta instills us and our surroundings with these qualities. This high-caliber prosperity is accompanied by love for liberty and justice. It has zero tolerance for suppression and oppression. We no longer permit dark and destructive forces to govern our life. Furthermore, this prosperity is ever nurturing. It is accompanied by the power to digest and assimilate everything that providence provides. This phenomenon applies to every level of our existence. We are able to digest and assimilate our food. We are able to digest and assimilate everything we gather from our studies and our interactions with others. We are able to digest and assimilate our differences. As with healthy biota (*karisha*), even the by-products and waste matter of our thoughts, ideas, and material or spiritual achievements become the source of nourishment for others (SS 9).

The prosperity invoked by Sri Sukta is accompanied by three more qualities: fulfillment of our desires, materialization of our intentions, and truthfulness of our speech. In this prosperous atmosphere our desires bear fruit but have no binding effect because they are fully aligned with the divine will. In this atmosphere we are clear about our intentions, enthusiastic in executing them, and delighted when they materialize. They too are fully aligned with the divine will and so have no binding effect. This form of prosperity has no room for false promises. We say exactly what we mean. The power of truth ensures our words come true (SS 10).

Fertility is another defining attribute of the prosperity invoked by Sri Sukta. In this prosperous atmosphere, couples embrace parenthood in a wise and healthy manner. While growing joyfully, children emit joy (SS 11).

This prosperity is further accompanied by the capacity of water to support life. A society blessed with this form of prosperity perceives water as the source of life. As a steward of this gift of nature, it ensures the full preservation of water's purity and sweetness (SS 12). Furthermore, in a society blessed with this prosperity there is respect for philosophers and thinkers. People value innovative ideas even more than the objects created from those ideas (SS 12).

Four more qualities that accompany this unique prosperity are associated with the natural world: moisture in the soil and air, fullness in bodies of water, fullness of fertility and nourishment, and the blossoming of nature. The practice of Sri Sukta affects the soil's capacity to retain moisture. The practice also makes the moisture in both the soil and the air available to organisms that depend on moisture. The prosperity invoked by Sri Sukta has a direct bearing on all bodies of water: oceans, glaciers, rivers, lakes, ponds, and streams. This prosperity is characterized by the fullness of all bodies of water. It is also characterized by pervasive nourishment. Every aspect of nature—air, water, soil, vegetation, animals, and humans—is bathed in the subtle energy of nurturance. The soil becomes fertile, the air is full of vitality, and blossoms are aromatic and full of nectar. A unique luster on the leaves of plants and trees and a radiant glow on our skin announces the arrival of the goddess of abundance (SS 13).

The nurturing energy of moisture in the soil and air invoked through Sri Sukta causes the inherent strength in our body and mind to manifest. This nurturing energy drives away dryness in our relationships and brings our tender feelings to the surface. It creates an environment that actively supports sharing love and compassion. Furthermore, these tender feelings are protected by a disciplined and enlightened mind. We are guided by our inner intuition, which knows the difference between love and distraction, compassion and pity (SS 14).

Finally, the abundance engendered by Sri Sukta is stable and brings stability to our personal and interpersonal relationships. This abundance goes beyond the domain of material objects. In addition to material wealth, we share a socioeconomic prosperity marked by high-minded, loving, trustworthy kinsmen and friends; by a balanced web of life comprising wild and domesticated animals; and by a healthy biosphere (SS 15).

In summary, Sri Sukta brings both internal and external prosperity. Uninformed, casual seekers use Sri Sukta to overcome life's day-to-day problems: family discord, recurring business failures, job stress, persistent health concerns, fear of losing loved ones, and fear of death. Relatively more informed seekers use it to overcome problems caused by deficiencies in their own body and mind. But seekers steeped in a tantric understanding of life and higher reality practice Sri Sukta to attenuate and eventually eradicate their deep-rooted afflicting tendencies. They practice it to overcome self-destructive habits and behaviors, such as fear, doubt, anger, self-pity, and their inability to let go of painful memories. They practice it to awaken their power of will and determination.

Such seekers use the practice of Sri Sukta as a gateway to the treasury of divine providence buried in their own body and mind. They practice it to awaken and reclaim nature's abundant wealth and to nurture their awareness of the higher reality that provides protection and nourishment to the entire web of life. They practice Sri Sukta to cultivate unconditional selfless love in their relationships and to expand their understanding of achievement. They practice it with the intention of entering the realm of intuition, which is the source of all innovative ideas. In short, seekers steeped in a tantric awareness of life practice Sri Sukta to transform themselves into islands of excellence.

Constant Awareness of Omniscient Reality

The second key to unlocking the unimaginable power of Sri Sukta lies in remembering there is an omniscient reality. It was here before we were born and will remain after we are gone. We are intelligent beings, but in regard to our birth and existence in this world our intelligence amounts to naught. We know nothing about why and how we were conceived, what imbued the fetus with feelings, who guided the development of our organs and limbs, and who provided the initial impetus to breathe. Who is the keeper of our intelligence? Where does the brain get its power to train our physiology to comprehend and execute its intentions? How do the lessons learned from our past experiences return as we need them? What is the source of our enthusiasm, courage, ambition, willpower, determination, and power of discernment? What makes us believe we can know the unknown and take our worldly and spiritual quest to new heights?

There is a reality that guides our birth, initiates breathing, establishes a relationship between the heart and brain, executes the complex functions of our organs and limbs, infuses our heart with feelings, and empowers our mind to stretch its capacity and intuit what lies beyond our senses. The most familiar word for that reality is *Ishvara*. Sri Sukta calls this reality *Jatavedas*.

Jatavedas means "one who knows everything about those who are born and anything ever created." In other words, Jatavedas is the omniscient being. It is beginningless and endless. It pervades and permeates the world made of and governed by time and space. It is the container of the forces that execute the law of cause and effect. Why we are born, what we need to live, and why and when we must die are fully known to the omniscient being. It also knows what we need to live a fulfilling life, amass inner wealth, and return after death with greater wisdom and the capacity for an even more fulfilling life. Jatavedas is at the core of Sri Sukta. All fifteen mantras directly invoke Jatavedas and request this omniscient being to bring the goddess of inner prosperity to us or carry us to her.

According to tantric mythology, Sri Vidya is the epitome of absolute beauty and joy. She is Sri Mata, the fountain of highest goodness and auspiciousness. She is Sri Maharajni, the paramount queen of beatitude. She is Tripura, the presiding divinity of the triple world—the world of waking, dreaming, and deep sleep, and of earth, heaven, and the realm in between. She is our very core and the core of the universe. She is subtler than the subtlest. She is beyond the reach of our thought, speech, and action. We become aware of this nameless, formless, transcendental divinity only when she assumes a name and form compatible with the perceiving power of our mind and senses.

Sri Sukta is vested with the power to make this unmanifest reality manifest. Sri Sukta commands this power for two reasons. First, it provides the initial spark for the transcendent goddess of abundance and beatitude to become immanent by tapping into the primordial pool of the all-knowing, omniscient being, Jatavedas. Second, Sri Sukta upgrades the quality of our mind and senses so we can comprehend and embrace the goddess of abundance and beatitude filling our inner and outer worlds. It does this by invoking the guiding and nurturing power of Jatavedas inherent in every nook and cranny of our being.

The relationship between Jatavedas and Sri Vidya is like that of fire and its radiance. Jatavedas is sacred fire (*agni*) and Sri Vidya is its radiance. Radiance is intrinsic to fire. For example, the sun is a gigantic fireball. Certain properties of its radiance are healthy for us and others are not. Its radiance is pleasant at certain latitudes and almost unbearable at others. Some forms of life thrive in bright sun while others thrive where the sun's radiance is shaded. The fireball remains the same but the various shades of its radiance have different effects. So is the case with the sacred fire, Jatavedas Agni, and its radiance, Sri Vidya. Jatavedas is spontaneously and constantly emitting numberless rays of omniscience. The unique shade of omniscience that awakens and nourishes the conditions in which our inner peace, prosperity, and feelings of fulfillment thrive is Sri, or Sri Lakshmi. The practice of Sri Sukta invokes Jatavedas and requests it to shine that unique shade of omniscience on us, or to transport us to the realm lit by that specific radiance.

An understanding of the omniscience of the divine being is the foundation for the practice of Sri Sukta. This understanding fills our mind and heart with the conviction that there is a higher reality watching over us. Every aspect of our body and mind and the world around us is pervaded by the omniscience of the divine being. As this understanding matures into constant awareness, we no longer seek assurance from outside for we have found it within. This results in faith and trust in ourselves and in our inner companion, Jatavedas. This faith and trust sheds a new light on Sri Sukta and its relationship with us. Each mantra becomes a conduit for our interaction with Jatavedas. We communicate with Jatavedas Agni and its radiance, Sri Lakshmi, the goddess of inner prosperity, just as we communicate and interact with our loved ones. We are filled with confidence that the omniscient being is fully aware of our intent, and there is no need to look for a sign of her response. It is there always.

As the *Yoga Sutra* tells us, faith breathes life into our practice. It compels us to do our practice sincerely and vigorously. Practice grounded in faith, sincerity, and vigor awakens our retentive power. Retentive power is the force that keeps the importance of our practice in the forefront of our mind. We are aware of our practice even when we are not actually engaged in it. Conscious reinforcement of the practice and its importance wards off disturbances, distractions, and inertia, and leads the mind to a state of stillness. This in turn releases the fountain of intuitive wisdom, transforming our intellectual understanding of the omniscient being into feeling. This feeling then matures into constant awareness—our own ever-awake inner friend. It is with us during our practice and at all other times. In the presence of this friend, obstacles have no power to come close to us. We have all the resources conducive to a successful practice.

A Personal Bond with the Seers of Sri Sukta

Jatavedas Agni is the seer of all mantras, including the mantras of Sri Sukta. When we rise above the petty behaviors of our mind and senses; let go of our disturbing, distracting, and stupefying thoughts; acquire a clear, tranquil mind; and turn that tranquil mind inward, we discover both the cause of and the cure for our most subtle afflictions: ignorance, distorted self-identity, attachment, aversion, and fear. With methodical practice of meditation, we attenuate the influence of these afflictions on our mind and eventually either destroy them or transform them into a positive force. In the yoga tradition, this is known as samadhi or nirvana.

Samadhi is an immersive state in which we are no longer holding on to the awareness of our self as an individual being. We are fully absorbed in the limitless pool of primordial omniscience. In this state, we see the omniscient being through the eyes of her omniscience. This is what makes a highly accomplished yogi a "seer." In this respect, a seer is exactly what he sees. It is an indescribable state. While abiding in this state, we see, know, and experience exactly the way the omniscient being sees, knows, and experiences. Our feelings and intentions are exactly hers. We are cognizant of all the joy and sorrow in the world and yet remain untouched by it.

When we descend from this state propelled by divine will, the knowledge and experience of the omniscient being and the various shades of her omniscience descend with us. As the *Yoga Sutra* tells us, during this descent we reach a mysterious state of consciousness known as *dharma megha samadhi*. This state is laden with limitless knowledge of higher truth, yet the awareness of self-identity returns, filled now with the purity and effulgence of the omniscient being. Scriptures describe this state as "half here, half there." In this state, we are fully aware of our intrinsic oneness with the omniscient being; at the same time we see the objective world with all its strengths and follies.

A unique shade of the radiance of the omniscient being—compassion—encompasses our self-identity. Our consciousness is saturated with the compassion-driven divine will. We are thrilled with the realization that submitting ourselves to divine will is our dharma. In response to this spontaneous realization, the omniscient divine being reveals the treasure hidden deep in its unique radiance of compassion.

The revelation of this hidden treasure is the source of mantras, and the seer is the one to whom this treasure is revealed. In regard to Sri Sukta, the first and foremost seer is Dakshinamurti. Sages like Dakshinamurti are identical to Jatavedas, the pure, transcendental, omniscient being. They are immortal for they are no longer subject to death, decay, and destruction. The consciousness they embody is beyond time, space, and the law of cause and effect. They do not fit into our definition of number and gender. They are beyond our comprehension, and yet, driven by their sheer compassion, they penetrate our field of comprehension, allowing us to know them and feel their presence.

We know and feel them not through our own effort, but through their kindness. They are vested with the power to dispense the treasure they themselves have received from the most radiant omniscient being, Jatavedas. It is with their tongues we pray to Jatavedas. We receive the gift of inner prosperity with their hands. We understand the value of this gift with their minds. It is through their intelligence that we assimilate this gift into our being. According to the tradition, this is how we progress in our sadhana and reap its fruit in a timely manner.

In addition to Dakshinamurti, four other sages are also known as seers of Sri Sukta: Ananda, Kardama, Shrita, and Chiklita. All of them are described as direct extensions of the omniscient being, Jatavedas, and its radiance, Sri Lakshmi. The tradition documents a list of seventy-one masters who serve as conduits to transmit the knowledge and experience of the vast range of Sri Vidya, of which Sri Sukta is a part. These seventy-one masters constitute the Sri Vidya tradition (see Appendix B). For a long time these masters passed on the knowledge and practice of Sri Sukta directly to their students as part of the oral tradition. A few thousand years ago, Veda Vyasa, the twenty-first master of the tradition, compiled these mantras into the version of Sri Sukta we have today.

Establishing a personal bond with these sages is the third key to the successful practice of Sri Sukta. Establishing a personal bond with them, however, is somewhat tricky. These sages lived thousands of years ago. All we know about them is that they are part of a lineage that originated in the East. This much information does not evoke feelings strong enough to mature into love and devotion for these masters. What does evoke love and reverence for them is knowledge and understanding regarding their nonphysical existence.

They were once human, just as we are. Through divine grace and their relentless practice, they crossed the quagmire of attachment and delusion that binds us here. They reached the realm of absolute freedom and joy. They were rewarded with unrestricted will and the power of infallible intention. They surrendered both of these rewards to the divine will. At the earliest inkling of the divine will, they happily renounced the immersive state of samadhi and descended to the state of dharma megha samadhi. In this state, they were fully enveloped by the consummate radiance of compassion. Through the eye of this compassion they saw individual souls struggling to find their way to fulfillment and freedom. They saw guiding these souls as an opportunity to serve the divine will, and so they descended further. Armed with trustful surrender, they threw themselves into the torrent of samsara.

That is how they were born. Once again they labored to find everlasting joy and safety. When they found it, they shared it with their contemporaries. After leaving their physical body, they enjoy their immortality while abiding in the state of dharma megha samadhi. From that state they watch over us and confer their unconditional love and guidance through their sheer infallible power of intention. They are always connected to us. Our understanding that their unconditional love and guidance is showering on us incessantly helps us become a fit container for receiving and retaining their love and guidance. This is how we secure the third key for practicing Sri Sukta successfully.

The Exposition of Sri Sukta

I *pray to the sages Dakshinamurti, Ananda, Kardama, Shrita, and Chiklita, who embody the essence of Jatavedas, the omniscient being. I am grateful to you for filling my mind with the understanding that you are the radiance of the most radiant being. Your presence dispels the darkness of ignorance, enabling us to see life and its creator without distortion. At the dawn of this endeavor to expound the content and subtle intent of the cluster of mantras known as Sri Sukta, I pray I may see these mantras through your eyes and convey them through your intelligence.*

Sri Sukta is your gift to the world. You have appointed the masters of the tradition to guard this gift and dispense it in compliance with your will. I offer my gratitude to you, O Sages, for making me your instrument to deliver this gift to generations of seekers. I pray that through this writing I convey everything that needs to be conveyed and refrain from including anything that should be transmitted only through your direct guidance. Because Sri Sukta is a revelation emerging from a direct dialogue between you and Jatavedas, I seek your permission and blessings to elaborate on who Jatavedas is, where and how this dialogue took place, and why you requested Jatavedas to bring Sri Lakshmi, the goddess of inner prosperity, to us.

Jatavedas is all-pervading omniscient reality. It is pure being, beginningless and endless. The power of will, the power of knowledge, and the power of action are intrinsic to it. Anything ever born or created is within the range of its awareness. It touches and feels everything that exists, including time itself, yet remains untouched and unaffected. It is where all diversities, complexities, and possibilities converge and rest. All the manifest and unmanifest forces engaged in guiding, protecting, and nourishing the world have their source in this reality. The unimaginably subtle and potent waves of energy and consciousness that give unique shape and character to the phenomenal world, as well as to our mind, originate here. Like vapor from the ocean, the life force emerges from here and, following the law established and executed by this omniscient being, condenses itself in different times and places. That is how life takes form. That is how matter and consciousness are united and how nameless, formless souls come into being. We exist only because our existence is sustained by Jatavedas, the very source of life.

Nothing in the universe is more pervasive and powerful than the omniscient being. That is why scriptures say that without moving, it reaches everywhere, and without exerting any effort, accomplishes everything. What could be more pervasive than the omniscient Jatavedas, who, having created the universe, penetrates its every nook and cranny while simultaneously enveloping it? What little we know about this world is only due to the power of comprehension we have received from the omniscient being. Even the desire to unravel the mystery of the omniscient being springs from this primordial pool. It is the wonder of all wonders. For untold ages, people from all cultures have been trying to experience it—the source of existence itself.

The sages remind us that the fainter our knowledge of the

omniscient being, the poorer our understanding of life. We begin to perceive the world defined by success and failure, gain and loss, praise and criticism as more compelling than life and its creator. As this process gathers momentum, we busy ourselves investing life's resources in protecting the world defined by these pairs of opposites. We succumb to seemingly unstoppable likes and dislikes. We become employees of our desires. Deficient understanding of the omniscient being and our relationship with it forces our consciousness to shrink. Desires originating from a shrunken consciousness are petty. Not knowing anything better, we run after our petty desires. When we get what we desire, we are delighted and identify ourselves as achievers. But soon the charm of achievement wears off and we pursue another desire, then another, and another, until we have depleted the sap of life. When we fail to get what we desire, we identify ourselves as losers. This is painful, but as soon as the pain of feeling like a loser wears off, we make another attempt to get what we want, then another, until we are depleted.

The sages found this world of likes and dislikes unfulfilling. They made a concerted effort to discover a way of expanding the scope of their consciousness to encompass a vision of a much bigger world. In the process, they realized that as the nature of our desires is transformed, the vision of our world expands and the quality of our desires improves. The idea of achievement and failure, which once overwhelmed us, loses its luster. We no longer desire petty objects, but aspire instead to achieve something bigger and brighter. Our concept of fulfillment becomes more comprehensive and inclusive.

In the light of this realization, the sages made an attempt to purify their mind, upgrade their desires, expand their consciousness, and reach that immersive state where all conflicts, contradictions, doubts, and fears come to an end. In this state of realization, known as dharma megha samadhi, they were able to see the total range of their mental contents. They were able to see all their positive and negative tendencies. With the help of their highly purified and insightful mind, they detached themselves from all of those tendencies.

This left them with a mind that saw worldly achievements and experiences as neither pleasant or unpleasant, good or bad, desirable or undesirable. With this purified and insightful mind, they saw the objects of the world simply as a means for serving the divine will. They were humbled by the realization that the omniscient being has given them everything they need to fulfill its will. They were thrilled by the realization that life in the mortal world is not bondage. They saw how every experience brought them closer to the divine being, and they also saw how throughout this journey, the guiding, protecting, and nurturing grace of the divine had always accompanied them. This understanding transported them to the most exalted state of trustful surrender. Effort-driven practice dropped away and they were swept up in an all-inclusive immersive state. They transcended self-identity and became one with the omniscient being.

In this consummate state of oneness with the divine, these exceptional masters are no longer subject to time, space, number, gender, and the law of cause and effect. They are exactly what Jatavedas is. In reference to this state, these masters are immortal. They are beyond birth and death. They see both the manifest and unmanifest aspects of reality through the eyes of Jatavedas. They see creation and annihilation, birth and death, through the eyes of Jatavedas. They experience themselves as the radiance of the radiant being. Their love and compassion for souls still struggling for their fulfillment and freedom are an extension of Jatavedas' love and compassion for them. Their connection with the world is inseparable from Jatavedas' connection with the world. Whenever the omniscient being is moved by its inherent compassion, these sages are moved. Thus they return to this world.

The process of descending to this world follows the same pattern as the ascent. When the sages descend from the immersive state to the state of dharma megha samadhi, their highly purified, insightful mind comes with them. Even though the sense of duality has emerged, the state of oneness is not compromised. They are fully connected to their source, the omniscient being, yet are able to see what lies below.

While in that state, they see a world inhabited by people with restless and confused minds. They see people suffering from poverty, hunger, disease, and old age. They see people trying to find peace and happiness while relying on a mind afflicted with fear, greed, doubt, desire, anger, hatred, ego, and attachment. They see a world deficient in love, compassion, and kindness. They see a world where people in power recklessly abuse their power, where healthy people abuse their senses, where the rich abuse their riches, and where almost everyone abuses the natural world. They see everyone crave health, wealth, and prosperity, but by and large their methods of satisfying these cravings are self-defeating.

The sages know the cure for this pervasive suffering. They also know how constricted people's consciousness has become and thus how reliant they are on their untrained, undisciplined, outwardly running minds. Knowing people have little trust in themselves, and even less in divine providence, the sages resorted to divine providence, which they know is the fountain of clarity, strength, and power of discernment people need to acquire true health, wealth, and prosperity. Standing between duality and nonduality, between the chaotic world below and the perfectly still realm above, the sages reached out to the omniscient radiance. With the tongue of this radiance, the sages made a direct appeal to the omniscient being, Jatavedas, which in the present cycle of creation emerged as the cluster of sixteen mantras known as Sri Sukta. The first fifteen mantras constitute the main body, while the sixteenth tells us succinctly how to practice Sri Sukta. An exposition of each of the sixteen mantras follows.

MANTRA 1

हिरण्यवर्णां हरिणीं सुवर्णरजतस्रजाम् ।
चन्द्रां हिरण्मयीं लक्ष्मीं जातवेदो म आवह ॥१॥

hiraṇyavarṇām hariṇīm suvarṇarajatasrajām
candrām hiraṇmayīm lakṣmīm jātavedo ma āvaha ||1||

O Jatavedas, please carry me to or bring to me the Divine Mother Lakshmi, the supreme beauty, the goddess as resplendent as gold, garlanded with gold and silver, delightful as the moon—the essence of gold embodying all forms of prosperity.

hiraṇyavarṇām, the one who is as pure and resplendent as gold

hariṇīm, the beautiful, blossoming; the female deer (at one time, Lakshmi turned herself into a doe); the one who resides in Hari, Vishnu, or the one in whom Hari resides

suvarṇarajatasrajām, the one who is garlanded with gold and silver; the one who wears the garland of flowers made of, or as resplendent as, gold and silver

candrām, the moon; the one who is as cooling and soothing as moonlight

hiraṇmayīm, the one who is the embodiment of gold; the one who is molten gold—living prosperity

lakṣmīm, the goddess of prosperity; the divinity endowed with all auspiciousness and goodness

jātavedas, O Omniscient Fire; O Most Sacred Fire presiding over rituals

ma, to me

āvaha, bring her from every direction in every respect

O Jatavedas, please bring Lakshmi, the goddess of prosperity and fullness, to me. May I recognize and embrace her as *Hiranya-varna,* the radiance of your intrinsic omniscience, omnipotence, and omnipresence. Enlightened by this radiance, may I become aware of your seven manifestations. May I recognize you as *Sapta-jihva,* the divine being with seven flames, residing in me as seven *chakras* (centers of consciousness). Nourished by these seven flames, may I experience the full range of human potential. Guided by these seven flames, may I reach all seven realms of existence, recognize all seven churches, hear all seven bells, perceive all seven stars, sit at the feet of all seven sages, and enjoy being a resident of the island made of seven gems, surrounded by seven seas.

May Hiranyavarna Lakshmi, your intrinsic radiance, help me recognize you as *Havya-vahana,* the omniscient being who carries my prayer, meditation, and offerings to the intended place in a timely manner. May the resplendent Lakshmi infuse my mind with the understanding that it is you as Havya-vahana who transports my oblations to the realm of divine providence, where destiny is created. As digestive fire, you transport nutrients to all the cells, limbs, and organs of the body. You transport my meditation to the state of samadhi. You transport my mind to the seers of the mantras. You bring the love, affection, and good will of my loved ones to me, and you carry my love, affection, and good will to my loved ones.

May Hiranyavarna Lakshmi, your intrinsic radiance, help me recognize you as *Ashvodara,* the omniscient being who contains my mind and senses in its womb. May the resplendent Lakshmi enable me to comprehend that you are the primary source of love, care, protection, and nourishment for my mind and senses. May this understanding fill my mind and senses with self-trust and confidence in their power to heal and rejuvenate themselves. Guided by you,

O Jatavedas, may my mind explore the objects of the world and experience them in the most enlightened and fulfilling manner.

May Hiranyavarna Lakshmi, your intrinsic radiance, help me recognize you as *Vaishvanara,* the unique form of the life force that fills the nooks and crannies of my body, the earth, and the entire space encompassed by the sun's orbit. May I comprehend that you, as Vaishvanara, ordain and execute the law of change. O Jatavedas, may your intrinsic radiance enable me to foresee patterns of change and extract the best this change contains. May your radiance transform my negative, destructive thoughts and feelings into thoughts that are positive and constructive. Guided by the radiance of Lakshmi, may I engage in actions that fill the landscape of my mind with the power of will, determination, enthusiasm, and self-confidence.

May Hiranyavarna Lakshmi, your intrinsic radiance, help me recognize you, O Jatavedas, as *Kaumara-teja,* the omniscient being who emits the energy of joy and innocence. O Jatavedas, may your intrinsic radiance enable me to reclaim and retain the purity and spontaneity of my childhood. May I enjoy playing with the objects of the world, but once I have finishing playing with them, may they not linger in my mind. Guide me, O Jatavedas, so that I succeed in all my endeavors but consume only what my body and mind can digest and assimilate.

May Hiranyavarna Lakshmi, your intrinsic radiance, help me recognize you, O Jatavedas, as *Vishva-mukha,* the face or mouth of the universe. May I recognize your face in my face. When I eat and drink, may I remember that I am making an offering into your mouth. May I hear and heed you when you speak to me through the mouth of the world. May I comprehend the intention behind people's actions, and may I respond to their actions with full awareness that your will always prevails. The outcome of all actions ultimately ends up in your mouth. You digest and process those actions. The fruits of my actions come back to me as destiny. In essence, you are the creator of destiny. May I remain active in the world with full awareness that you are the creator and master of my destiny. In my destiny there is no room for frustration and disappointment, for your love for me is unconditional and you know how to design a destiny for me that carries the gift of lasting fulfillment and ultimate freedom.

May Hiranyavarna Lakshmi, your intrinsic radiance, help me recognize you as *Deva-mukha,* the mouth of celestial beings. Celestial beings receive their nourishment when offerings are made into your mouth. Celestial beings also serve as your mouth. You accept my offerings when they are made into the mouth of celestial beings. Celestial beings are also your mouthpiece—you speak to me through them. I pray that these celestial beings transmit their guiding radiance only in proportion to my current capacity to withstand it. May their guiding radiance expand the scope of my consciousness so that I can comfortably assimilate the ever-increasing intensity of their radiance. May the radiant grace of the sages become the doorway to knowing your essence, O Jatavedas. May your guiding grace enable me to recognize and embrace the most resplendent Hiranyavarna Lakshmi so I may seek and find prosperity that is at once auspicious, beautiful, and dignified.

O Jatavedas, please bring Lakshmi, the goddess of prosperity and fullness, to me. May I recognize and embrace her as *Harini,* the divinity adored by Hari, the master of Sri Vidya and the protector of, and provider for, all living beings. May the Divine Mother Lakshmi infuse my mind with the qualities of a vigilant deer that is constantly on the move in search of green and tender pastures. Guided and nourished by her energy, may I be free from sloth and inertia. May I not fall victim to complacency. Unhindered by deep valleys and steep hills, may I traverse all terrains of life with the clear objective of reaching a safe place abounding in nourishment. I know her company brings inner prosperity, and worldly prosperity follows. O Jatavedas, I pray I may invest both my inner and outer prosperity to serve a higher cause—serving all living beings who Sri Hari loves as his own children.

O Jatavedas, please bring Lakshmi, the goddess of prosperity and fullness, to me. May I recognize and embrace her as *Suvarna-rajata-sraja,* the goddess wearing a garland of silver and gold. May this unique form of radiance upgrade my taste and thus inspire me to extract and acquire that which is best in my surroundings and in me. May the inner prosperity mobilized by the goddess Lakshmi awaken my sense of aesthetics. May I appreciate that which is good and beautiful in me and that which is good and beautiful in others. May my thought, speech, and action carry the luster of the Divine Mother Lakshmi, whose radiance outshines the luster of all precious gems and metals.

O Jatavedas, please bring Lakshmi, the goddess of prosperity and fullness, to me. May I recognize and embrace her as *Chandra,* the lunar energy that cools my aggressive tendencies. May your intrinsic omniscience fill my mind with peace, enabling me to think and speak in a kind and loving manner. May my actions reflect the equanimity of my mind. May I not be a threat to anyone; may I not see anyone as a threat to me.

O Jatavedas, please bring Lakshmi, the goddess of prosperity and fullness, to me. May I recognize and embrace her as *Hiranmayi,* the resplendent goddess with no tolerance for darkness. May her radiance empower me to conceive a philosophy of life that affords no room for low-grade thoughts, beliefs, and ambitions. Living under the guidance and protection of Hiranmayi Lakshmi, the resplendent goddess of prosperity, frees me from feelings of unworthiness, empowering me to design my life in a manner befitting her standards.

MANTRA 2

तां म आवह जातवेदो लक्ष्मीमनपगामिनीम् ।
यस्यां हिरण्यं विन्देयं गामश्वं पुरुषानहम् ॥ २ ॥

tām ma āvaha jātavedo lakṣmīmanapagāminīm
yasyām hiraṇyam vindeyam gāmaśvam puruṣānaham
||2||

O Jatavedas, please carry me to or bring to me the Divine Mother Lakshmi, the one who once having come never goes away. In her may I obtain gold, cows, horses, and manpower.

tām, to her
ma, to me
āvaha, bring her from every direction in every respect
jātavedas, O Omniscient Fire; O Most Sacred Fire presiding over rituals
lakṣmīm, the goddess of prosperity; the divinity endowed with all auspiciousness and goodness
anapagāminīm, the one who does not go away
yasyām, in the one in whom
hiraṇyam, gold
vindeyam, derived from the verb *vid*, to obtain; may I obtain
gām, cows
aśvam, horses
puruṣān, humans; manpower
aham, I

O Jatavedas, as I stand between you and the world below, I see a bitter reality. The world of humans is rife with anxiety and disappointment. People work to collect worldly objects. They identify those objects as wealth and work hard to protect them, and yet hardly anyone succeeds in protecting their wealth for a significant length of time. The pain of losing one's wealth is much more intense than the pain involved in earning it. O Omniscient Being, you have chosen me as a conduit to transmit your unconditional love and compassion to human beings sincerely engaged in finding lasting fulfillment and ultimate freedom. I pray to you, O Jatavedaṣ, to shed your radiance on them so that they can understand the difference between short-lived prosperity and prosperity that lasts.

O Jatavedas, please bring Lakshmi, the goddess of prosperity and fullness, to me. May I recognize and embrace her as *Anapagamini,* prosperity that having once come never goes away. May I pass this recognition on to those who doubt their ability to achieve what they need and are fearful of losing what they have achieved. May I mantrically capture the recognition that wealth that does not illuminate our mind and expand our consciousness is not worth calling wealth. May the wealth I gather from your radiance be filled with illumination. May it shine like *hiranya,* molten gold. May the wealth I collect from your radiance hold value, as gold holds value. May the wealth emitted by your omniscience manifest as cows and horses and as the humans who love and care for them. May I pass on this resplendent gift of prosperity to mankind; may they receive it, treasure it, and use it wisely.

O Jatavedas, may the radiance of your omniscience enable people to see what I see through your eyes. Acquiring a stable and discerning mind is lasting wealth. I clearly see how a stable and discerning mind brings stability in every aspect of life. With the stable and discerning mind you gave to me, I see why you created the animal kingdom—why you made some animals untrainable, thus keeping them closer to the natural world, and why you made others trainable, so they can be domesticated. Similarly, I see why you created humans with a broad range of tastes and interests. I see the symbiotic relationship between humans and the natural world and between individuals and communities embodying different sets of skills. May your intrinsic radiance enable humans to see what I see. Riding waves of mantric revelation, may the stable and discerning Lakshmi walk into the lives of those seeking stable prosperity.

MANTRA 3

अश्वपूर्वां रथमध्यां हस्तिनादप्रबोधिनीम् ।
श्रियं देवीं उपह्वये श्रीर्मा देवी जुषताम् ॥३॥

aśvapūrvām rathamadhyām hastinādaprabodhinīm
śriyam devīm upahvaye śrīrmā devī juṣatām ||3||

I invoke Sri [the Divine Mother Sri Vidya], along with her retinue, with horses in the front and a chariot in the center; her arrival is announced by *nada*, the trumpeting of elephants. May Devi, the shining being, engage me in her service as she pleases.

aśvapūrvām, the one who has horses in front
rathamadhyām, the one who has a chariot in the middle
hastinādaprabodhinīm, the one who awakens [us] with the trumpeting of elephants
śriyam, the Divine Mother Sri Vidya; the goddess of beauty and bliss
devīm, the Devi; the shining being
upahvaye, I invoke
śrīḥ, the Divine Mother Sri Vidya
ma, to me
devī, the shining being
juṣatām, be pleased

O Jatavedas, I am a wave of your intrinsic radiance. You are my mother, father, guide, protector, and the provider of nourishment. My unblemished mind and its retentive power are gifts from you.

Because of these gifts, I know your intention behind my descent to this world. You have chosen me to deliver your gifts of enthusiasm, courage, inquisitiveness, and ambition to the world inhabited by humans—qualities they need to extract the wealth hidden in their own thought, speech, and action, as well as in the world around them.

O Jatavedas, please bring Lakshmi, the goddess of prosperity and fullness, to me. May I recognize and embrace her as the epitome of power, glamour, and dignity. May I see her as the supreme luminary. Her arrival must not go unheralded. May nature's forces announce her advent. I see her coming to me seated in her chariot (*ratha-madhya*), with horses gamboling and prancing in front (*ashva-purva*) and trumpeting elephants (*hasti-nada-prabodhini*) bringing up the rear. May I serve your will, O Jatavedas, by proclaiming her arrival. May my words embodying the mantric power of your omniscience enable seekers of prosperity and fullness to see and embrace the queen of beauty and goodness in the way I do.

MANTRA 4

कां सोस्मितां हिरण्यप्राकारां आर्द्रां ज्वलन्तीं तृप्तां तर्पयन्तीम् ।
पद्मे स्थितां पद्मवर्णां तामिहोपह्वये श्रियम् ॥४॥

kām sosmitām hiraṇyaprākārām ārdrām
jvalantīm tṛptām tarpayantīm
padme sthitām padmavarṇām tāmihopahvaye śriyam ||4||

I invoke Sri [the Divine Mother Sri Vidya], who is the creative intelligence of the creator, whose countenance has a slight smile, who is surrounded by a wall of gold; the one who is moist, the one who is lustrous, the one who is content, the one who confers contentment, the one who is seated on the lotus, the one who is identical to the lotus.

kām, the creative intelligence of the creator
sosmitām, with a hint of a smile
hiraṇyaprākārām, the one who is surrounded by a wall of gold
ārdrām, the moist one
jvalantīm, the radiant being
tṛptām, the one who is content
tarpayantīm, the one who grants contentment
padme sthitām, the one who sits on the lotus
padmavarṇām, the one who is identical to the lotus
tām, to that [Sri]
iha, here
upahvaye, I invoke
śriyam, the Divine Mother Sri Vidya; the goddess of beauty and bliss

O Jatavedas, please bring Lakshmi, the goddess of prosperity and fullness, to me. May I recognize and embrace her as *Ka,* the creative intelligence of the creator. May my mind be blessed with creativity and innovative ideas. May every aspect of creation unveil the creative intelligence of the creator. May the Divine Mother Lakshmi, as Ka, the force of creativity, enable me to extract nature's abundance.

O Jatavedas, please bring Lakshmi, the goddess of prosperity and fullness, to me. May I recognize and embrace her as *Sosmita,* the goddess of beauty and joy with a smile on her face. May the prosperity brought by her bring a smile to my face and the faces of those around me. May the prosperity engendered by her presence be free of pain and sorrow. May the acquisition of wealth not incur pain for others, and may it not hurt or harm my conscience.

O Jatavedas, please bring Lakshmi, the goddess of prosperity and fullness, to me. May I recognize and embrace her as *Hiranyaprakara,* the goddess surrounded by a wall of gold. May the safeguards protecting my wealth be as pure and illumined as gold. May there be transparency in what I earn and possess. May the power of transparency and truth nullify people's efforts to usurp that which rightfully belongs to me. May the consequences of even my negative karmas fail to steal or stain the gift of wealth I receive from the Divine Mother Lakshmi.

O Jatavedas, please bring Lakshmi, the goddess of prosperity and fullness, to me. May I recognize and embrace her as *Ardra,* the divinity bathed in the waters of love and compassion. May I become fully cognizant of the needs and functions of my body, mind, and senses. May the wealth received from the Divine Mother Lakshmi as Ardra irrigate and nourish my body, mind, and senses. May my wealth nourish the tender feelings of my heart, and may my sensitivity to others grow as my wealth grows.

O Jatavedas, please bring Lakshmi, the goddess of prosperity and fullness, to me. May I recognize and embrace her as *Jvalanti*, a fully lit fire. May the gift of wealth brought by this unique form of Lakshmi be free of smoke. May this gift further illuminate my life and the lives of those who share this gift.

O Jatavedas, please bring Lakshmi, the goddess of prosperity and fullness, to me. May I recognize and embrace her as *Tripta*, the embodiment of contentment. May the process of acquiring wealth and claiming ownership of it be accompanied by contentment. May I be free from anxiety and fear while I am engaged in finding my inner and outer wealth. Once I have found it, may I remain free of the fear of losing it. May I be grateful for what I have achieved, and may I remain inspired to achieve all that I need for the next level of my unfoldment.

O Jatavedas, please bring Lakshmi, the goddess of prosperity and fullness, to me. May I recognize and embrace her as *Tarpayanti*, the divinity conferring contentment. Guided by this form of Lakshmi, may I be instrumental in bringing contentment to the lives of others. May I have the ability to extend my spiritual and worldly prosperity to the world at large, and may everyone experience the same degree of peace and contentment as I do.

O Jatavedas, please bring Lakshmi, the goddess of prosperity and fullness, to me. May I recognize and embrace her as *Padmesthita*, the divinity seated on the lotus. Looking through the radiance of your eyes, O Jatavedas, may I see the Divine Mother Lakshmi seated on the lotus of my life. She presides over all my thoughts, feelings, and sentiments. Because of her my eyes see, my ears hear, my nostrils smell, my tongue tastes, and my skin perceives touch. Because of her my mind thinks and my intellect discerns. Following her will, the seven centers of consciousness (chakras) blossom in my energy body. May I experience one and only one all-pervading shakti, Lakshmi, residing in all seven chakras, from the region of the perineum all the way to the crown. May I experience her as the power of stability at my perineum, the power of passion in my pelvic region, the power of self-confidence at my navel center, the power of love and compassion at my heart center, the power of creativity and aesthetic expression at my throat center, the power of decisiveness and discernment at the center of my forehead, and the power that enables us to experience our oneness with you at my crown.

O Jatavedas, please bring Lakshmi, the goddess of prosperity and fullness, to me. May I recognize and embrace her as *Padma-varna,* the one identical to the lotus. May the revelation of Lakshmi as Padma-varna enable me to understand that the lotus of my life is a direct manifestation of your omniscience. I am intelligent because your omniscience shines in me. I have feelings because your intention shines in me. My sense of *asmita*, I-am-ness, lit by your dualistic intelligence makes me feel that there are seven different centers of consciousness in me. But when I see through the eye of your all-pervading immersive intelligence, all seven centers of consciousness are extensions of your omniscience. You are these seven centers of consciousness. There is no difference between you and what issues from you. Standing between you and the phenomenal world below, I pray that the realization that there is no difference between you and the world issuing from you becomes my wealth. I also pray that those who seek your guidance using these revealed words receive, retain, and assimilate the gift of inner prosperity just as I have.

MANTRA 5

चन्द्रां प्रभासां यशसा ज्वलन्तीं श्रियं लोके
देवजुष्टामुदाराम् ।
ताम् पद्मिनीमीं शरणं प्रपद्ये अलक्ष्मीर् मे नश्यतां त्वां
वृणोमि ॥५॥

candrām prabhāsām yaśasā jvalantīm śriyam loke
devajuṣṭāmudārām
tām padminīm īm śaraṇam prapadye alakṣmīr me
naśyatām tvām vṛṇomi ||5||

I take refuge in Sri, who is delightful, uniquely lit, shining with glory, revered and attended by luminous beings, and known in the world through her generosity. I take refuge in that Sri who embodies the lotus and who as the sound *īm* forms the core of the seed mantra of Sri Lakshmi. May my inner and outer poverty be destroyed.

candrām, the one who is as delightful as the moon
prabhāsām, the resplendent one
yaśasā, with glory
jvalantīm, the glowing one
śriyam, the Divine Mother Sri Vidya
loke, in the world
devajuṣṭām, revered and attended by luminous beings
udārām, the one who is generous
tām, to that [Sri]
padminīm, the one who embodies the lotus, sits on the lotus, or wears lotus garlands

īm, shakti mantra forming the core of *hrīm*, the *bija* mantra of Sri Lakshmi
śaraṇam, refuge; shelter
prapadye, I surrender
alakṣmīḥ, lack of prosperity; lack of wealth; lack of beauty and goodness
me, my
naśyatām, be destroyed
tvām, you (to you)
vṛṇomi, I embrace; I choose

O Jatavedas, please bring Lakshmi, the goddess of prosperity and fullness, to me. May I recognize and embrace her as *Chandra,* the embodiment of delight. May I remain aware of her presence at the *sahasrara chakra*, the crown center. O Jatavedas, you are the primordial fire of consciousness. An infinite number of rays radiate from you. Your blessed children, like myself, perceive a range of rays that are delightful and nurturing. I call that aspect of your radiance *Chandra-kala.* Like a glacial snow it melts at the sahasrara chakra, irrigating all systems of the body and all faculties of the mind with its ambrosia. May the ambrosia of Chandra-kala fill me with passion for life. May it nourish my body, mind, and senses. May I pass on this passion and nourishment to human beings, who are always in need of love, compassion, patience, the capacity for forgiveness, and overall inner healing and rejuvenation.

O Jatavedas, please bring Lakshmi, the goddess of prosperity and fullness, to me. May I recognize and embrace her as *Prabhasa,* the wave of radiance. As the wave of radiance, may the Divine Mother Lakshmi dispel the darkness of ignorance, ego, confusion, attachment, and fear. May the prosperity she brings prevent me from groping in darkness. May it prevent me from pushing others into darkness. May Prabhasa, the queen of inner radiance, guide me to reinvest her gift of abundance in the most illuminating manner, which yields lasting peace and happiness.

O Jatavedas, please bring Lakshmi, the goddess of prosperity and fullness, to me. May I recognize and embrace her as *Jvalanti,* the one glowing with her intrinsic magnificence (*yashasa*). May the Divine Mother Lakshmi as Jvalanti give a spark to the kundalini shakti lying dormant in me. May the spark of Jvalanti awaken the inherent potential of all seven chakras. May this glowing goddess bring my higher qualities to light, and may others understand me. May she bring the higher qualities of others to light, and may I understand others. May she bring nature's abundance to light. May I carry the gift of her abundance to the world, and may the world treasure her gift diligently.

O Jatavedas, please bring Lakshmi, the goddess of prosperity and fullness, to me. May I recognize and embrace her as *Devajushta,* the divinity revered and attended by devas, luminous beings. O Omniscient and Omnipotent Being, you created three realms: earth, heaven, and the space that stands in between. As the omnipresent being, you reside in all three realms, preside over them, and transcend them altogether. As a wave of your luminosity, I stand in the middle realm. I see what is above me; I see what is below me; I see what is within me; and I see what is outside me. May I absorb the Divine Mother Lakshmi, revere her as my own essence, and attend her as her most sincere and trusted child. As I take physical form, may she make my body and mind her residence. May she walk and talk as I walk and talk in the world. May the mortal beings hear and feel her presence in the reverberation of revealed words.

O Jatavedas, please bring Lakshmi, the goddess of prosperity and fullness, to me. May I recognize and embrace her as *Udara,* fully manifest and active prosperity. Nature is the container of limitless abundance, but most of it lies dormant. To those not fully bathed in your radiance, O Jatavedas, the dormant abundance is imperceptible and inconceivable. May the Divine Mother Lakshmi as Udara shake off the dormancy of nature's abundance and make it perceivable, so that people with limited knowledge and comprehension can gain access to nature's bounty. May the goddess of active prosperity infuse the minds and hearts of seekers with generosity.

O Jatavedas, please bring Lakshmi, the goddess of prosperity and fullness, to me. May I recognize and embrace her as *Padmini,* the shakti that gave birth to the first lotus. I know who, at the end of the annihilation era of the universe (*pralaya*), captured the highly diffuse pervasiveness and concentrated it at the navel center of Vishnu, the divinity who rules over all-pervading time and space. I know how, from this concentrated time and space, the lotus of the universe was born, how the blossom gave birth to the creator and definition to time and space; thus the nonexistent came into existence. It is Padmini shakti, your intrinsic radiance and the mother of seven states of consciousness, who dwells in Vishnu as yogic sleep (*yoga nidra*), in Brahma as the power of awakening (*jagara*), and in me as knowledge (*veda-garbha*). She is the essence of both the creator and the creation. May my consciousness be in full view of the mother of the primordial lotus, and guided by you, O Jatavedas, may I deliver the nectar of this lotus to seekers.

O Jatavedas, please bring Lakshmi, the goddess of prosperity and fullness, to me. May I recognize and embrace her as *im,* the heart and soul of the Sri Vidya mantra. May the Divine Mother Lakshmi walk into my life in the form of the bija mantra *hrim.* May *im*, the soul of the bija *hrim*, illuminate and activate the wealth contained in *hrim*. May this mysterious mantra hold the power of knowledge (*aim*) and the power of will (*klim*) on either side. May the mantra *hrim* hold and sustain my three states of consciousness (waking, dreaming, and deep sleep), just as it holds and sustains the three peaks of the fifteen-syllable Sri Vidya mantra. O Jatavedas, I surrender myself to this most mysterious radiance of yours. May I have no room for anyone or anything other than the Divine Mother Lakshmi. I choose her and only her.

MANTRA 6

आदित्यवर्णे तपसोऽधिजातो वनस्पतिस्तव वृक्षोऽथ बिल्वः ।
तस्य फलानि तपसानुदन्तु यान्तरा याश्च बाह्या अलक्ष्मीः ॥६॥

ādityavarṇe tapaso'dhijāto vanaspatistava vṛkṣo'tha bilvaḥ
tasya phalāni tapasānudantu yāntarā yāśca bāhyā alakṣmīḥ ||6||

O Sun-bright Divinity, the Bilva tree, the lord of the forest, is born from your *tapas*. Through *tapas* one attains the fruits of that tree. Please drive away all my internal and external destitution.

ādityavarṇe, O Sun-bright Divinity
tapasaḥ, from tapas
adhijataḥ, that has been born
vanaspatis, the lord of the forest
tava, your
vṛkṣaḥ, tree
atha, a word denoting auspiciousness
bilvaḥ, Bilva tree (*Aegle marmelos*)
tasya, of that
phalāni, fruits
tapasā, with tapas; through tapas
nudantu, to remove
yā, that which

antarā, internal
yāśca, and that which
bāhyā, external
alakṣmīḥ, lack of prosperity; lack of goodness and beauty

O Jatavedas, I am grateful to you for giving me the knowledge pertaining to the origin of the Bilva tree. In the beginning, vegetation covered the earth. It was populated by insects and by animals that consumed vegetation. Trees were devoid of fruit. Propelled by your compassionate intention, the Divine Mother Lakshmi decided to create an environment conducive to humans. She committed herself to intense austerity. Through the power of her austerity she condensed her essence with such intensity that she began to glow like the sun. From that radiance emerged the Bilva, the first tree to bear fruit. From the eyes of the Divine Mother Lakshmi emerged Kama Deva, the lord of absolute beauty, and Rati, the goddess of passion. At the behest of Lakshmi, this pair made the Bilva tree their home. At this, the brightly lit moon of beauty and joy began to shine over the forest covering the earth, transforming it into a garden fit for human habitation. Since then all forces of creation have revered the Bilva tree as the lord of the forest.

O Jatavedas, may my knowledge of the Bilva tree—its origin, its relationship with the Divine Mother Lakshmi, its healing and nourishing properties, its alchemical power to transform base metals into gold, and its spiritual power to transform a dull and dense mind into a radiant one—enable human beings to recognize and treasure the Divine Mother's gift. May humans commit themselves to tapas, practices through which they detoxify their body and purify their mind. With their pure and discerning mind, may humans understand that under the rule of the Bilva tree the natural world has the capacity to provide everything they need to live a healthy, happy, and prosperous life. May humans be committed to tapas, the practices through which they become more vigilant and enlightened. May they commit themselves to tapas, practices through which they achieve *sankalpa siddhi,* infallible power of will and determination. May they understand that only through tapas can they receive, retain, and multiply the gifts the Divine Mother Lakshmi pulled from her subtle domain and materialized in the external world for their sake. O Jatavedas, may this illuminating knowledge drive away both external and internal poverty.

MANTRA 7

उपैतु मां देवसखः कीर्तिश्च मणिना सह ।
प्रादुर्भूतोऽस्मि राष्ट्रेऽस्मिन् कीर्तिमृद्धिं ददातु मे ॥७॥

upaitu mām devasakhaḥ kīrtiśca maṇinā saha
prādurbhūto'smi rāṣṭre'smin kīrtimṛddhim
dadātu me ||7||

May the friend of deva, the bright being accompanied by Kirti and Mani, come to me. I am born in this land. Please bless me with glory and wealth.

upaitu, please come
mām, to me
devasakhaḥ, friend of deva, the bright being; friend of Rudra, embodiment of the life force
kīrtiḥ, glory; the quality that makes one glorious; the power that accompanies glory
ca, and
maṇinā, with Mani, more precisely Chintamani, the wish-fulfilling gem; or with Manibhadra, the divine being who gives access to the celestial wealth
saha, with
prādurbhūtaḥ, have been born
asmi, I am
rāṣṭre, in a country; belonging to a country
asmin, in this
kīrtim, glory
ṛddhim, wealth
dadātu me, give me

O Jatavedas, *ritam*, the unbending governing law of nature, emerged from your kind intention and gave definition to the truth. In the light of this truth, seven sages emerged. One of the seven, Pulastya, has Vishrava, "the well-heard one," as his son. Vishrava is known for his power and wisdom, as well as for the patience needed to contain and share that power and wisdom. Vishrava begot a son who instantly earned the ever-lasting friendship of Rudra Deva, the divinity embodying the radiant life force. Thus the seers of truth call him *Deva-sakha,* friend of the deva. This friend of the radiant life force, as the unbending law of nature dictates, is the lord of heavenly wealth. This lord of heavenly wealth designs destiny, which determines how long one may live, in what type of body, and what desirable or undesirable circumstances one will face. O Jatavedas, may this lord of heavenly wealth, the best friend of the life force, come to me while accompanied by his two distinguished aides, Kirti and Mani.

May the arrival of the lord of heavenly wealth fill my mind and heart with heavenly virtues—love, kindness, compassion, forgiveness, fortitude, and the courage to share and give. May I bask in the power and wisdom he has inherited from his father Vishrava. May I be able to contain and share that power and wisdom. May I always remember that the sage Pulastya is the grandsire of the lord of heavenly wealth and my grandsire as well. By virtue of my connection with my grandsire, my origin is in truth, which itself is defined by none other than the unbending law of nature. May this truth enable me to bathe in the radiance of Kirti, the distinguished aide of Deva-sakha, the lord of heavenly wealth.

O Jatavedas, as a human I am designed to have the desire for recognition. Honoring that design, I pray that the lord of life may come to me with Kirti, the glory that commands recognition. I also pray that glory may come with Mani, the self-shining gem of power and discernment. May the arrival of the lord of heavenly wealth—accompanied by Kirti, glory, and Mani, self-shining power and discernment—enable me to remain grounded in the principle of trustful surrender.

O Jatavedas, I have descended to the world of humans. I am part of the land in which I am born. I take part in the destiny of those around me. The joy and sorrow of this world is my joy and sorrow. In service of your will I remain firm in my resolve: this world is my home and serving it is my dharma. For this reason, O Jatavedas, I pray you may give me glorious wealth and those who hear this proclamation may cherish this wealth.

MANTRA 8

क्षुत्पिपासामलां ज्येष्ठामलक्ष्मीं नाशयाम्यहम् ।
अभूतिमसमृद्धिञ्च सर्वां निर्णुद मे गृहात् ॥८॥

kṣutpipāsāmalām jyeṣṭhāmalakṣmīm nāśayāmyaham
abhūtimasamṛddhiñca sarvām nirṇuda me gṛhāt ||8||

I eliminate hunger, thirst, impurity, decrepitude, and poverty. Please remove all forms of emptiness and poverty from my home.

kṣut, hunger
pipāsā, thirst
malām, impurity; toxin; uncleanliness
jyeṣṭhām, the phenomenon of decrepitude; the one who was born before Lakshmi
alakṣmīm, lack of prosperity; lack of goodness and beauty
nāśayāmi, I destroy
aham, I
abhūtim, lack of fullness
asamṛddhiñ, lack of prosperity
ca, and
sarvām, all
nirṇuda, remove
me, my
gṛhāt, from home

O Jatavedas, Omniscient Divine Being, while standing between you and the world of humans, I resolve to use your gift of glorious wealth to exterminate *kshut,* hunger. Nature is the repository of abundance and yet there is hunger. Some are hungry because they do not have enough to eat. Others are hungry because they do not have the ability to digest what they eat. Some are hungry for love, others for violence. Some are hungry for sensory stimulation, and others for peace. Some are not satisfied with what they have and are hungry for what others have. Some are suffering from ideological hunger, and others from spiritual hunger. In the natural world, the soil is hungry for water and the plants are hungry for nutrients. May the wealth I have received from you, O Jatavedas, drive all shades of hunger away from my home—the world in which I live.

I see pervasive thirst in the world in which I reside. Some are suffering because they do not have enough to drink, and others because they do not have the ability to drink. Some are suffering from sense cravings, either because they do not have access to sensory objects or because their senses are so weak and frail they cannot enjoy sensory objects. Some are thirsty for knowledge but have no access to it, while others have access to it but no motivation to collect and use it. The mind is thirsty for clarity of thought, and the heart for unconditional love. Communities thirst for mutual respect, and individuals for personal freedom and empowerment. The soil is thirsty for timely rain, and the rivers for clean, abundant water. May the wealth I have received from you, O Jatavedas, drive all shades of thirst away from my home—the world in which I live.

O Jatavedas, Omniscient Divine Being, while standing between you and the world of humans, I resolve to use your gift of glorious wealth to remove *mala*, impurity, which is clogging the systems of humans and the natural world. You designed the human body as your temple and the inner chamber of the heart as your altar. But I now see this beautiful temple filled with toxins and the altar buried in sorrow and regret. Toxins are filling the space both outside and inside the body. Natural sources of nourishment—air, water, and food—have become contaminated. The body's internal ecology is also out of balance. Imbalanced and sluggish bodily systems are holding on to waste matter. Confused and careless minds are holding on to wasteful thoughts. Communities and individuals are caught in a vicious cycle of blame. May the wealth I have received from you, O Jatavedas, drive all shades of impurity from my home—the world in which I live.

O Jatavedas, Omniscient Divine Being, while standing between you and the world of humans, I resolve to use your gift of glorious wealth to exterminate *jyeshtha,* decrepitude. In the world of mortals I see people lacking trust in themselves, trust in their loved ones, trust in justice, and trust in divine providence. Yet they fail to see how this lack of trust causes them to become mentally decrepit. The lack of trust forces them to alienate themselves from others. Alienation leads to loneliness. Even surrounded by family and friends, they feel lonely. This accelerates aging, and a decrepit mind fails to do anything about it. A decrepit mind and accelerated aging are in complete contrast to the beauty and joy that accompanies the Divine Mother Lakshmi. A decrepit mind and accelerated aging fill human minds and hearts with *alakshmi,* conditions that oppose beauty, joy, and abundance. O Jatavedas, as I prepare to walk into my new home—the world of mortals—I pray that the wealth I have received from you drives all shades of decrepitude (*jyeshtha*) and conditions that oppose beauty, joy, and abundance (*alakshmi*) from my new home.

O Jatavedas, Omniscient Divine Being, while standing between you and the world of humans, I see how destitution is manifesting in many different forms in the world of mortals. In some places it is manifesting as a lack of tools and means to find prosperity. In other places, the means are available but people lack the knowledge or will to use them to find prosperity. Some are suffering because they have nothing or very little in their home. Others have everything in their home but are suffering because their heart is empty. At the advent of my journey to the world of mortals, I resolve to use your glorious wealth to exterminate all forms of poverty and emptiness.

MANTRA 9

गन्धद्वारां दुराधर्षां नित्यपुष्टां करीषिणीम् ।
ईश्वरीं सर्वभूतानां तामिहोपह्वये श्रियम् ॥९॥

gandhadvārām durādharṣām nityapuṣṭām karīṣiṇīm
īśvarīm sarvabhūtānām tāmihopahvaye śriyam ||9||

I invoke the Divine Mother Sri, who is the gateway to inner fragrance, who is invincible and eternally nurturing. I invoke the Divine Mother Sri, who embodies the power of will and the power of action, the one who is lord of all living beings.

gandhadvārām, the gateway to fragrance
durādharṣām, unstoppable; invincible
nityapuṣṭām, eternally nurturing; the source of eternal nourishment
karīṣiṇīm, embodiment of the power of will and action; the force that propels the entire process of consuming food—all the way to eliminating waste
īśvarīm, the power of omniscience; the intrinsic omniscience of the omniscient being; might of the almighty
sarva, all
bhūtānām, of living beings
tām, to that [Sri]
iha, here
upahvaye, I invoke
śriyam, the Divine Mother Sri Vidya; the goddess of beauty and bliss

O Jatavedas, I invoke the Divine Mother Sri Lakshmi, who is *Gandha-dvara,* the gateway to inner fragrance. There is no greater wonder than the truth that she is *gandha,* fragrance, as well as *dvara,* the gateway to her own intrinsic fragrance. How can I express the joy of my realization that numberless waves of omniscience and omnipotence arise from you? Time and space arise from these waves. In the realm of time and space an infinite number of universes arise. They too are the waves of your omniscience and omnipotence.

Out of those numberless waves, Brahma, the embodiment of your creativity, gathers 360 of them. *Tvashta,* the celestial builder, selects five of those waves to fashion the phenomenal world. From the wave infused with the power of sound, he creates the sky; from the wave infused with the power of touch, he creates air; from the wave infused with the power of visibility, he creates fire; from the wave infused with the power of wetness, he creates water; and from the wave infused with the power of smell, he creates earth, solid matter. This cluster of five elements—space, air, fire, water, and solid matter—comes to life only when the Divine Mother Sri Lakshmi penetrates the earth and enlivens it with her aroma. Forms emerge and names are assigned. The universe of galaxies and the earth, which is the habitat of mortals, receive discrete identities. O Jatavedas, may the people I am assigned to serve understand that the numberless shades of aroma the soil exudes is the aroma of Sri Lakshmi. Sri Lakshmi is the soul of earth, water, fire, air, and space. O Jatavedas, she is as omnipresent as you are.

O Jatavedas, I am eternally grateful to the radiance of your omniscience, Sri Lakshmi, who avails herself to humans by manifesting as turmeric (*gandha*). Turmeric is her body and she is turmeric's soul. I invoke the goddess of inner prosperity, beauty, and joy. May you, Divine Mother Lakshmi, unleash your healing and rejuvenating power hidden in turmeric. May your essence become the gateway (*dvara*) to my physical, mental, and spiritual well-being, as well as the doorway to the well-being of those who hear these words.

O Gandha-dvara, the embodiment of and gateway to inner fragrance, may you bring the seer of the *maha mrityunjaya* mantra and motivate him to unleash its mantric power, particularly *sugandhim*, the finest of all fragrances. May the sugandhim portion of the maha mrityunjaya mantra destroy foul smell, bitter speech, and negative thoughts. May you become the gateway to the maha mrityunjaya mantra, and may you elevate my consciousness so I embody you and thus exude the elixir of longevity contained in the maha mrityunjaya mantra.

O Jatavedas, Omniscient Being, I invoke the Divine Mother Sri as *Duradharsha,* the invincible force. Without her, the creator cannot gather the materials to create. Without her, the protector and provider cannot gather the tools and means to protect what is created. Without her, the lord of change cannot deconstruct and introduce change. I invoke Sri Lakshmi, the fundamental principle of abundance, which propels the process and phenomena of creation, maintenance, deconstruction, and renovation. Come to me, O Duradharsha, the irrepressible divinity, and join me in my journey in the world of mortals so I can serve them to your full satisfaction.

O Jatavedas, I invoke the Divine Mother Sri as *Nitya-pushta*, the embodiment of lasting nourishment. The power of nourishment and sustainability pervades every nook and cranny of the universe. This power is present in a speck of dust and in a mighty star. It exists in every part of the natural world, humans included. Only when people become disconnected from this inexhaustible source of nourishment, or when it becomes dormant, do aging, decay, and death ensue.

O Nitya-pushta, the embodiment of lasting nourishment, may you bring with you the seer of the maha mrityunjaya mantra and motivate him to unleash its mantric power, particularly *pushti vardhanam,* the power that expands the domain of nourishment beyond the constraints of physical reality. May the pushti vardhanam portion of the maha mrityunjaya mantra remove the conditions that cause physical, mental, and spiritual decay. May the power of the maha mrityunjaya mantra be subsumed in you. May I embody you and thus exude the elixir of longevity contained in the maha mrityunjaya mantra.

O Jatavedas, Omniscient Being, I invoke the Divine Mother Sri as *Karishini,* the power of action and will. As *Kari,* you are the true doer because you are the power of action. When you mobilize your inherent potential, the inner reality begins to manifest in the external world. Imperceptible tools and means become visible. The dormant desire for worldly achievement and spiritual success awakens and becomes active. So potent is your power of action that theoretical knowledge begins to seek concrete expression; scientific concepts are transformed into applied sciences; the dormant sense of aesthetics is transformed into the performing arts; and imagination becomes innovation. O Primordial Force of Pulsation (*Kari*), please join me in my journey to the world of mortals. May your presence enable people to shake off their age-old inertia. Please put them on the path of action. May humans commit themselves to self-effort. Please motivate humans to cast off the stiff shroud of mental conditioning. May they renounce their slavery to the past and begin to live actively and fully in the present.

O Divine Mother, as *Ishini* you are the power of will and determination. At your will, the power of action begins to pulsate and the actor begins to act. Your way is always the way—paths follow you. Sensing your inclination, destiny changes its course. You are *Sankalpa,* the power of intention inherent in Brahma, the creator. You are *Dhatri,* the power of nourishment inherent in Vishnu, the provider and protector. You are *Prakriti,* the ever-changing force inherent in Shiva. Together you are Ishini, the autonomous power to do what you wish to do, the power to be free from doing what you do not wish to do, and the power to undo whatever has been done. O Boundless Might of the Almighty, I bow to the unconditional love, kindness, and generosity that prompt you to live in the finite vessel of body and mind. That is how humans received such a perceptive and discerning mind. You dwell in all in the form of the power of indomitable will and discernment (*buddhi*). May humans recognize and revere this truth.

Because of you as Kari, the power of action, and Ishini, the power of will and determination, there is action and that action has purpose. Every aspect of creation is constantly performing action and every action is purposeful. Every part of the body and mind is engaged in purposeful action. As long as humans are aware of their timeless connection with you, they remain engaged in purposeful action. Their thought, speech, and action flow effortlessly and purposefully. They instinctively know what to consume and how much to consume, what to retain and what to get rid of, what to remember and what to forget, what to say and what to refrain from saying. O Fundamental Force of Transformation (*Karishini*), join me in my journey in the world of mortals so that I can serve your will to your full satisfaction.

O Jatavedas, Omniscient Being, I invoke the Divine Mother Lakshmi as *Ishvari,* your intrinsic shakti who presides over the entire sentient and insentient world. The whole world is integral to her self-awareness. She lives in all yet is known only to a few fortunate ones. Seated deep in the heart of living beings, she determines how much knowledge and memory they are to be granted. People caught in the torrent of samsara have a limited capacity to face and process all the contents of their mind. Seeing everything stored in their mind can overwhelm those not fully absorbed in her. Thus she kindly puts a veil over the vast field of memory and illuminates only that which they can use to find the *summum bonum* of life—lasting fulfillment and ultimate freedom. Today I invoke this aspect of your shakti and pray that she accompanies me to the world of mortals so that in her light people make the best use of their knowledge and memory and continue expanding the scope of their consciousness.

O Jatavedas, standing between you and the world of mortals I resolve to serve as a conduit for your Ishvari shakti. May this shakti enable people to shed *avidya,* ignorance; *asmita*, distorted self-identity; *raga*, attachment; *dvesha*, aversion; and *abhinivesha*, fear. May they learn the art of living in the world and yet remaining above it. May people embrace this shakti as their inner guide, and may this inner guide enable them to discover the best in themselves and the best in others.

MANTRA 10

मनसः काममाकूतिं वाचः सत्यमशीमहि ।
पशूनां रूपमन्नस्य मयि श्रीः श्रयतां यशः ॥१०॥

manasaḥ kāmamākūtim vācaḥ satyamaśīmahi
paśūnām rūpamannasya mayi śrīḥ śrayatām yaśaḥ
||10||

May I achieve the objects of my desire. May my intentions materialize. May my speech be truthful. May I acquire the full range of cattle and grain. May the Divine Mother Sri and the glory that accompanies her find a home in me.

manasaḥ, of mind; related to the mind
kāmam, desire
ākūtim, intention
vācaḥ, speech
satyam, truth
aśīmahi, may I achieve
paśūnām, of cattle; pertaining to cattle
rūpam, form; essence
annasya, of grain
mayi, in me
śrīḥ, Sri; the Divine Mother; the goddess
śrayatām, may it reside
yaśaḥ, glory; fame

O Jatavedas, Omniscient Being, during my ascent to you I lost all my mental contents. I do not even have a mind—I am simply a wave of your radiance. I lack specificity and without that I cannot interact with those who have a concrete identity. Please give me an identity compatible with those whom I serve. Furthermore, I am utterly bereft of ignorance, self-identity, attachment, aversion, and fear—the group of afflictions that rules the world of mortals. I do not know how to live and act in a world dominated by these afflictions. Please give me a mind and fill it with your thoughts and intentions. Guide that mind to descend into a body that serves your purpose. While living in that body, may I learn the skills to identify my desires and translate them into action. May my actions enable people to identify their own desires and translate them into action. May my actions bear fruit—helping and serving those striving to find fulfillment in life.

O Jatavedas, your intentions are my intentions. They guide my thought, speech, and action. While living in the world of mortals, may I remain aware of the source of my intentions and the power that drives them. In full view of this awareness, may I live in the world and strive to achieve what it has to offer. May my intentions and the actions propelled by them bear fruit. May that fruit serve your will.

O Jatavedas, may my words always come true. May I never make false promises or utter a prayer I do not mean wholeheartedly. May my words conform to my thoughts, and may my actions conform to my words. May the revelations coming from you remain pure and be expressed by pure tongues. May my words transmit your essence to all those who hear them.

O Jatavedas, Omniscient Being, the entire universe is before my eyes. With few exceptions, most of it is sterile. The earth is an exceptional place, for in it endless diversity abounds. It is home to an unimaginably vast range of insects and animals. These creatures vary widely in appetite and behavior yet all serve a common purpose—helping humans to thrive and find their freedom and fulfillment. Human well-being depends on the diversity and well-being of animals, both wild and domesticated. The well-being of the animal kingdom depends on the well-being of insects and the world of vegetation. O Jatavedas, standing between you and the world of mortals, I pray that the Divine Mother Lakshmi may create conditions conducive to the health and well-being of animals, the link between humans and the rest of creation. May I have the full range of animals at my disposal. May there be no deformity in them. May their limbs and organs be fully formed. May they contribute to a balanced ecology, and may that balanced ecology help them serve humans well.

O Jatavedas, may my home—the world of mortals—be filled with food. May the intelligence you have deposited in humans enable them to understand that nothing in the world is as important as food. Life depends on food. Lack of food leads to death. Food deficient in nutrients leads to a slow death. Anticipation of not having enough food causes anxiety and fear, which drains clarity and calmness of mind. Living from hand to mouth obliterates the passion for life. O Jatavedas, fill my newfound home with nutritious food in abundance. More important, fill my kinsmen's minds and hearts with respect for food and give them the motivation to share with those who are deprived of food. This way, O Jatavedas, bring the Divine Mother Sri and the glory that accompanies her to me. May she reside with me in my newfound home, the world of mortals.

MANTRA 11

कर्दमेन प्रजा भूता मयि संभव कर्दम ।
श्रियं वासय मे कुले मातरं पद्ममालिनीम् ॥११॥

kardamena prajā bhūtā mayi sambhava kardama
śriyam vāsaya me kule mātaram padmamālinīm ||11||

O Sri, with the birth of Sage Kardama you became a mother. O Kardama, you live in me. Also, please invite Mother Sri, wearing a garland of lotuses, to live in my family.

kardamena, through Sage Kardama; because of Sage Kardama
prajā, unique birth-giver
bhūtā, living beings
mayi, in me
sambhava, be born
kardama, O Sage Kardama
śriyam, the Divine Mother Sri Vidya; the goddess of beauty and bliss
vāsaya, making to dwell
me, my
kule, in the family; in the lineage
mātaram, mother
padmamālinīm, the one who is the embodiment of, or garlanded with, lotuses

O Jatavedas, Omniscient Being, how fortunate I am that as I cast my glance over my new home, the world of mortals, you are bringing the knowledge of the sage Kardama to the forefront of my consciousness. The shortcomings of this world and the people who inhabit it no longer concern me for I know who Sage Kardama is, what his relationship is with you, and how the finer forces of nature respond to his presence. He is your reflection; he is what you are. Because he emerged before time and space were born, he is your eldest son. Because he emerged the instant you thought of him, the sages address him as Sadyojata, "born instantly." Because Kardama emerged from your intrinsic radiance, he is the son of Sri Lakshmi. He mirrors his mother in beauty and joy. I offer my obeisance to this great soul for whom the unmanifest goddess of inner joy and abundance assumed motherhood, thus becoming manifest to all creation. My homage to Kardama, who is always accompanied by his mother, Sri Lakshmi.

O Jatavedas, I thank you for revealing the details of Kardama's life. He is married to Devahuti, the force who transports fire offerings to the celestial realm. She herself is the daughter of Manu, the collective consciousness of the human race. Thus Kardama is the anchor for all human endeavors. In union with his consort, Devahuti, he ensures human endeavors bear fruit. Standing at the juncture of unmanifest and manifest reality, I pray: Please, Kardama, come and live in the world of mortals, my new home.

O Jatavedas, how I thank you for revealing that Kardama and Devahuti brought Kapila, the lord of *siddhas*, to this world. Standing in full view of your inner radiance, O Jatavedas, I hear Kapila imparting the knowledge and practice of meditation on the lotus of the heart to his own mother, Devahuti. I also hear Kapila transmitting the knowledge of Sankhya Yoga to the *brahma rishis*. I am fully aware of the knowledge that enables humans to distinguish right from wrong, good from bad, and useful from useless. O Jatavedas, I am grateful to you, your son Kardama, and your grandson Kapila for giving me this knowledge. Guided by your will, may I find the space inside and outside me filled with the presence of Kardama's entire grand family as I enter the world of mortals.

O Sage Kardama, please do everything necessary to induce the Divine Mother Lakshmi as *Padma-malini* to reside in my family. In the presence of Padma-malini, the divinity who wears a garland of lotuses, may all the chakras—the lotuses in my body—blossom. May she make my body her home; may she make my family and lineage her home; may she make all the *kula tattvas*, the building blocks of my body and mind in the phenomenal world, her home. In the form of discerning power, may she penetrate every nook and cranny of my being, enabling me to discover her loving and guiding grace in everything and everyone. In short, may my home become her home, and may I live in her home as her child. May the power of this revelation help mortals gain access to the courtyard of Kardama's household.

MANTRA 12

आपः सृजन्तु स्निग्धानि चिक्लीत वस मे गृहे ।
नि च देवीं मातरं श्रियं वासय मे कुले ॥१२॥

āpaḥ sṛjantu snigdhāni ciklīta vasa me gṛhe
ni ca devīm mātaram śriyam vāsaya me kule ||12||

O Presiding Deity of the Waters, create an atmosphere of love and affection. O Chiklita, son of Divine Mother Sri, please dwell in my home. Furthermore, please invite the Divine Mother Sri to dwell in my family and lineage.

āpaḥ, waters
sṛjantu, please create
snigdhāni, loving; affectionate
ciklīta, a sage
vasa, live
me, my
gṛhe, in the house
ni, completely; fully
ca, and
devīm, the devi; the shining being
mātaram, mother
śriyam, the Divine Mother Sri Vidya; the goddess of beauty and bliss
vāsaya, making to dwell
me, my
kule, in the family; in the lineage

O Jatavedas, standing between you and the world of mortals I invoke the subtle forces of the waters. May the waters of the oceans, rivers, and lakes unveil their subtle properties. May water as glacial ice and clouds bring peace and prosperity to the world. May the waters supply nourishment to all forms of life. May the subtle nutrients contained in water nourish the mind as well as the body. May water bring forward the sweetness and bonding capacity (*snigdhani*) of the mind. May it drive away mental dryness and fill the mind with sensitivity toward others. May people share water instead of fighting over it. For this reason, O Jatavedas, I invoke Chiklita, the blessed son of the Divine Mother Lakshmi.

I invite you, O Chiklita, to live with me in my new home. Like Kardama, the Divine Mother held you in her womb. She rocked you in her arms and played with you in her courtyard—so great is your unsurpassed fortune. She passed her genius and ingenuity on to you. Thus you came to be known as Chiklita, the embodiment of genius and ingenuity.

Without your help, O Chiklita, humans will not see water as anything more than an object of consumption. They will not see how the body shrivels when deficient in water, or how the natural world withers and civilizations vanish. O Chiklita, your active presence in my new home will guide my kinsmen, the human race. Under the influence of the genius you embody, they will see water as more than a commodity and will aspire to discover its spiritual value.

I know that the Divine Mother is wherever you are, and yet I request you to formally invite her to live in my newfound home. Even though my home is small and inhabited by people with small minds and small aspirations—conditions not fit to accommodate her grandeur—your presence will nullify these conditions. In the presence of Sri Lakshmi and you, the world of mortals will be transformed into a paradise. The scope of people's consciousness will expand; they will rise above their petty concerns. They will have less interest in short-lived gratification and more interest in making this world a better place. With this conviction, O Chiklita, I invite you to my home along with the Divine Mother Sri Lakshmi.

MANTRA 13

आर्द्रां पुष्करिणीं पुष्टिं पिङ्गलां पद्ममालिनीम् ।
चन्द्रां हिरण्मयीं लक्ष्मीं जातवेदो म आवह ॥१३॥

ārdrām puṣkariṇīm puṣṭim piṅgalām padmamālinīm
candrām hiraṇmayīm lakṣmīm jātavedo ma āvaha
||13||

O Jatavedas, please carry me to or bring to me the Divine Mother Lakshmi, who is wet, who presides over lakes and ponds, who is the source of nourishment, who embodies the color of newness, who wears a garland of lotuses, who is as delightful as the moon, and who is as radiant as gold.

ārdrām, wet
puṣkariṇīm, lakes and ponds
puṣṭim, nourishment; source of nourishment
piṅgalām, pinkish color, the color of newness
padmamālinīm, the one who wears the garland of lotuses
candrām, the one who embodies the shakti of the moon
hiraṇmayīm, the one who is the embodiment of gold; the one who is bright like molten gold
lakṣmīm, the goddess of prosperity; the divinity endowed with all auspiciousness and goodness
jātavedas, O Omniscient Fire; O Most Sacred Fire presiding over rituals
ma, to me
āvaha, bring her from every direction in every respect

O Jatavedas, Omniscient Being, I invoke the Divine Mother Sri as *Ardra,* the divinity of wetness. I know that Ardra is the unique radiance of your life-giving love and compassion. In the vast sky, she resides in her highest concentration in the region corresponding to the sixth constellation of stars. That is why the sages named that constellation Ardra. Just as your omniscience moistens the human mind and intellect with intelligence, Ardra moistens the sixth constellation with the power of wetness, allowing water to manifest in the way mortals experience it. She is the soul of water. She fills the atmosphere with moisture. At her behest, clouds are formed and oceans created. Ardra flows in the veins and arteries of all living beings. In response to her subtle feelings, hormones are secreted. Tears of joy and sorrow are her reflections. In her presence, life thrives; in her absence, it withers. O Jatavedas, bring the Divine Mother Sri as Ardra to me, for only under her protection and guidance can I succeed in serving your will.

O Jatavedas, Omniscient Being, I invoke the Divine Mother Sri as *Pushkarini,* the divinity who presides over ponds and lakes. May ponds and lakes be filled with water. May mortals realize ponds and lakes are integral to the web of life—they are vessels of life. May mortals also recognize the ponds and lakes in their own body. Every cell is a pond and every organ a lake. May these vital ponds and lakes be filled with the waters of Sri as Pushkarini. May human beings cultivate a mind refined enough to sense the energetic counterparts of these vital ponds and lakes. Through their refined mind, may they bathe in the lake of the senses located in the pelvic region, as well as in the lake of discernment located in the region corresponding to the center of the forehead. Please bring this goddess of ponds and lakes to me, for only under her protection and guidance can I succeed in serving your will.

O Jatavedas, Omniscient Being, I invoke the Divine Mother

Sri as *Pushti,* the embodiment of nourishment. May the Divine Mother Sri as Pushti fill my inner and outer worlds. May she create a nurturing environment in the world outside me and inside me. May nature exude her nurturing shakti. May my body, mind, and senses exude the power of nourishment. I pray to the Divine Mother Sri as Pushti because I know only under her protection and guidance can I succeed in serving your will.

O Jatavedas, Omniscient Being, I invoke the Divine Mother Sri as *Pingala,* the one who embodies the color of newness. May the Divine Mother Sri as Pingala fill my inner and outer surroundings with the energy of newness. May I see her emanation in the smooth, glowing skin of children and in the quickness of their minds. May I see her in the shine on new leaves and feel her presence in the freshness of the air. May I experience her as my ability to let go of the past, my determination to live in the present, and my enthusiasm for envisioning a bright future. I pray to the Divine Mother Sri as Pingala, the goddess of newness, because I know under her protection and guidance I can succeed in serving your will—pulling mortals out of their dead, dark past.

O Jatavedas, Omniscient Being, I invoke the Divine Mother Sri as *Padma-malini,* as *Chandra,* and as *Hiranmayi.* As Padma-malini may she make all seven lotuses (*padma*) in my energy body into a garland (*mala*). May there be no disconnection between the different chakras—centers of consciousness—in me. May the energy manifesting in a particular chakra add beauty and joy to the other chakras. As Chandra (the moon), may the Divine Mother Sri remove harshness from me, replacing it with tenderness. As Hiranmayi (embodiment of gold), may she transform my base tendencies and bring forward my pure and pristine self, which mirrors your radiance. O Jatavedas, I request you to bring the Divine Mother Lakshmi as Padma-malini, Chandra, and

Hiranmayi to me, because I know that in order to serve you well, all the lotuses (chakras) must blossom and be strung into a garland; in my thought, speech, and action I must be pleasant; and I must be grounded in my pure and pristine self. Please keep these different forms of Mother Lakshmi in my full view so that I can make your treasury available to the mortals whom I am destined to serve.

MANTRA 14

आर्द्रां यः करिणीं यष्टिं सुवर्णां हेममालिनीम् ।
सूर्यां हिरण्मयीं लक्ष्मीं जातवेदो म आवह ॥१४॥

ārdrām yaḥ kariṇīm yaṣṭim suvarṇām hemamālinīm
sūryām hiraṇmayīm lakṣmīm jātavedo ma āvaha ||14||

O Jatavedas, please carry me to or bring to me the Divine Mother Lakshmi, who is wet, who embodies the power of action, who embodies the power of restraint, who is resplendent like gold and wears a necklace of gold. O Jatavedas, please carry me to or bring to me the Divine Mother Lakshmi, who is the essence of the sun and as radiant as gold.

ārdrām, wet
yaḥ, the one who is
kariṇīm, embodiment of the power of action
yaṣṭim, staff symbolizing restraint; embodiment of the power of restraint
suvarṇām, resplendent like gold
hemamālinīm, the one who wears a necklace of gold
sūryām, the one who is the essence of, or the shakti of, the sun
hiraṇmayīm, the one who is the embodiment of gold; the one who is molten gold—living prosperity
lakṣmīm, the goddess of prosperity; the divinity endowed with all auspiciousness and goodness
jātavedas, O Omniscient Fire; O Most Sacred Fire presiding over rituals
ma, to me
āvaha, bring her from every direction in every respect

O Jatavedas, Omniscient Being, once again I invoke the Divine Mother Sri as *Ardra,* the divinity of wetness. Please irrigate my body, mind, and senses with the nurturing waters of your love, kindness, and compassion. The more I prosper in the world, the more loving, kind, and compassionate I become. As I walk among mortals, may they become aware that insensitivity toward others invites inner poverty. May Ardra, your radiance, fill my mind and heart with sensitivity toward others, leading to the awakening of amity for those who are happy and compassion for those who are suffering.

O Jatavedas, Omniscient Being, once again I invoke the Divine Mother Sri as *Karini,* the divinity who embodies the power of action. By looking through the lens of your omniscience, I have seen that Karini is *spanda,* the timeless pulsation of your will. As it pulsates, dormant forces of the universe awaken. Once again, the unmanifest finds itself on the path of manifestation. Vishnu shuns his yoga nidra, Brahma unleashes his creativity, and Shiva rises from samadhi.

O Jatavedas, as Ishvara you become the container of your Karini shakti, the limitlessly pulsating power of action. At that stage, the sages proclaim your name as Kari and your shakti as Karini. As Kari, you are the doer, and as Karini, you are the power of doing. I bow to you and the shakti intrinsic to you. May the power of this revelation destroy the inertia that forces humans to remain loyal to ignorance and inaction. May the Divine Mother Sri as Karini guide me on the path of action so I may serve your will.

O Jatavedas, Omniscient Being, I invoke the Divine Mother Sri as *Yashti,* the power of restraint. Yashti is your unique self-guided, self-controlled wave of omniscience. Just as omniscience is intrinsic to you, the power of restraint is intrinsic to your omniscience. She is the law and the enforcer of the law. Because of her, the sun illuminates—but does not incinerate—the world of mortals. Obeying the command of Yashti, the planets stay in their orbits, the oceans rise and fall within their boundaries, the seasons cycle in turn, and the law of karma prevails. May the Divine Mother Sri as Yashti, the power of restraint, give me the insight and strength to stay on the path assigned by you, O Jatavedas. May this power enable me and those I serve to exercise the privilege you have granted to achieve lasting peace and happiness.

O Jatavedas, Omniscient Being, I invoke the Divine Mother Sri as *Suvarna,* as *Hema-malini,* as *Surya,* and as *Hiranmayi.* The Divine Mother Sri is formless and nameless, yet for the sake of mortals she assumes form. Because the form she assumes emits light, the sages address her as Suvarna. May the self-luminous Suvarna fill my inner and outer worlds with the light of knowledge and understanding. Because the jewelry she wears is made of gold, the sages address her as Hema-malini. May Hema-malini, the divinity decked with gold, fill my mind with superior thoughts and my life in the external world with wealth worthy of admiration. Because she embodies the life-giving power of the sun, the sages call her Surya. May Surya banish the darkness of the past as the sun banishes night. Because the Divine Mother Sri is the epitome of the power of revelation, the sages call her Hiranmayi, the embodiment of inner illumination. May the illuminating power of Hiranmayi enable me to know all that is worthy of knowing. O Jatavedas, may I become the container of the mantric essence of Suvarna, Hema-malini, Surya, and Hiranmayi, and may I deliver that essence to the world of mortals. May the people in that world receive, retain, and multiply this essence.

MANTRA 15

तां म आवह जातवेदो लक्ष्मीमनपगामिनीम् ।
यस्यां हिरण्यं प्रभूतं गावो दास्योऽश्वान् विन्देयं
पुरुषानहम् ॥१५॥

tām ma āvaha jātavedo lakṣmīmanapagāminīm
yasyām hiraṇyam prabhūtam gāvo dāsyo'śvān
vindeyam puruṣānaham ||15||

O Jatavedas, please carry me to or bring to me the Divine Mother Lakshmi, the one who having once come never goes away. In her may I obtain plentiful gold, cows, helpers, horses, and the company of humans.

tām, that
ma, to me
āvaha, bring her from every direction in every respect
jātavedas, O Omniscient Fire; O Most Sacred Fire presiding over rituals
lakṣmīm, the goddess of prosperity; the divinity endowed with all auspiciousness and goodness
anapagāminīm, the one who does not go away
yasyām, in the one in whom
hiraṇyam, gold
prabhūtam, plenty; abundant
gāvo, cows
dāsyaḥ, helpers; assistance; manpower
aśvān, horses
vindeyam, may I acquire

puruṣān, humans; human company
aham, I

O Jatavedas, Omniscient Being, once again for my own sake I affirm your omniscience as intrinsic to you. Because of your intrinsic omniscience, you know how unsurpassed is your omnipresence and omnipotence. In you lies the seed of perfection. Nothing in the world is equal to you. You are your own locus. You are the only reality. You are the knower, the knowable, and the process of knowing. You are the wonder of all wonders. Time and space emerge as you glance at yourself. The law of cause and effect emerges as you play. Creation is an outpouring of your inner content. How can anyone other than you comprehend your grandeur? Yet I experience your all-pervading beginningless and endless presence as a wave of your intrinsic radiance. I know you, because as the power of knowing you are in me and you are me. Your irrepressible and infallible will gives me a distinct identity. I hear my name proclaimed by you. I understand my dharma assigned by you. I stand in the space bordered on one side by duality and on the other side by nonduality. From here you are in my full view and so is your creation. Propelled by your will, I resolve to descend from here to the world of mortals.

Through the eyes of your omniscience, I see how profound your love is for your creation and for those who inhabit it. The love of your intrinsic radiance, the Divine Mother Lakshmi, who fills the nooks and crannies of this creation, is unconditional and boundless. Yet I see a bitter reality: in regard to humans, her company is cyclical and short-lived. In the earliest part of people's lives, she lives with them as innocence, playfulness, spontaneity, and agility. Soon she is gone, leaving only a faint trace. When she returns, she brings the gifts of charm, passion, vitality, vigor, ambition, and assertiveness. Then she leaves again and her gifts mostly vanish in her absence. This cyclical coming and going of the queen of beauty and joy continues until mortals breathe their last. In between, they have interludes of success and failure, pleasure and pain, honor and humiliation, satisfaction and disappointment. These interludes are totally dependent on when and how Sri Lakshmi, the goddess of inner prosperity, comes and goes. O Jatavedas, since you have appointed me to serve your mortal children, I pray that you bring the Divine Mother Sri to me with the promise that, once having come, she will not leave me. May I walk in the world of mortals with that Divine Mother Sri who never shuns those whom she has once blessed with her presence.

I also see another bitter reality: people have formed the habit of comparing their fortunes with the fortunes of others. Their joy in having what they have is contaminated by the pain of seeing that others have more. Mortals volunteer to be victims of jealousy, never realizing that jealousy is the mother of destitution. For those afflicted with jealousy, nothing is enough, and yet, O Jatavedas, they deserve your love and compassion more than those who are free of such afflictions. May the goddess of fortune prevail, and may that same goddess guide mortals to renounce their jealousy and enjoy the abundant gifts of providence (*prabhutam*).

O Jatavedas, as I stand between you and the world below, I see mortals suffering from self-created misery. They are in the habit of placing their trust in imaginary wealth rather than in actual wealth. Gold is actual wealth. It is one of the most durable metals. Luster is its inherent property. No other metal enhances beauty as much as gold. It diminishes neither in quality nor quantity, even after changing hands repeatedly. The medicinal properties of gold are unequaled. If understood well and used properly, gold can help mortals restore their spiritual luster, lifting their consciousness to experience their oneness with you. That is why gold is the supreme holder of value—actual wealth.

And yet, mortals delight in creating and accumulating objects that are often harmful to them and to the world in which they live. Such materials are perceived as wealth. To substantiate this perception, they keep adding endless layers of imaginary value. Because deep within they know that the wealth they value so much rests on the quicksand of collective imagination, mortals live in constant fear that it will vanish. I pray to you, O Jatavedas, please bring Sri Lakshmi to me, who in nature manifests as gold. May the goddess of inner prosperity enable humans to understand the value of gold and its proper application. May they comprehend the true meaning of the "golden age" and be inspired to embrace it.

O Jatavedas, please shed your radiance on mortals so they can understand that the golden age is marked by a golden mind. With the rise of a golden mind, the darkness of ignorance disappears: People see the difference between what is truly good and what is merely pleasant. They see the difference between self-respect and vanity. They understand what to accumulate and when, and also what to renounce and when. A golden mind is the abode of all forms of wealth, for a golden mind is the most befitting home of the Divine Mother Sri. O Jatavedas, please bless me with a golden mind, and bless my mortal kinsmen with the capacity to comprehend the radiant wealth of Lakshmi contained in me and thus be inspired to cultivate a golden mind.

O Jatavedas, I am certain that with their perceptive golden minds my kinsmen will recognize that the animal kingdom is their wealth and will prize the symbiotic relationship between humans and animals. The health and happiness of humans is closely associated with the health and well-being of animals.

Every creature big or small is part of the web of life. Every member of the animal kingdom is constantly engaged in serving the web of life. From their vantage point at the top of the food chain, may humans see how animals serve each other in a mutually supportive manner, and how the entire animal kingdom serves humans. May humans understand they are not the owners of the animal kingdom but the caretakers. May these caretakers be blessed with plentiful cows and horses and the rest of the animal kingdom. May this kingdom be their wealth, and may they protect, nourish, and use their wealth wisely.

O Jatavedas, using their perceptive, golden minds, may my kinsmen treat each other with love and respect. Diversity is part of nature's design. There is a reason for the differences in people's skills, talents, tastes, and interests. Humans are imperfect but have the capacity to become perfect. Life is an opportunity to discover and expand this capacity. This opportunity materializes when human beings unite their skills, talents, tastes, and interests to work toward a common goal: helping each other find lasting fulfillment and freedom. They can work toward this common goal only when they rise above their sense of inferiority and superiority and share the fruits of their collective endeavors lovingly and selflessly. O Jatavedas, free my mortal kinsmen from the arrogance that often accompanies power and position. May my kinsmen be blessed with plentiful helpers, friends, and colleagues, and may they treasure each other's company.

MANTRA 16

यः शुचिः प्रयतो भूत्वा जुहुयादाज्यमन्वहम् ।
श्रियः पञ्चदशर्चं च श्रीकामः सततं जपेत् ॥१६॥

yaḥ śuciḥ prayato bhūtvā juhuyād ājyamanvaham
śriyaḥ pañcadaśarcam ca śrīkāmaḥ satatam japet ||16||

An aspirant desiring to receive the grace of the Divine Mother Sri should recite the fifteen mantras of Sri Sukta and should make the offering of ghee daily with purity and vigilance.

yaḥ, the one who
śuciḥ, clean
prayataḥ, vigilant
bhūtvā, upon becoming
juhuyād, should offer oblation
ājyam, of ghee
anvaham, every day
śriyaḥ, of Sri
pañcadaśarcam, the sukta consisting of fifteen mantras
ca, and
śrīkāmaḥ, desirous of Sri
satatam, without interruption
japet, should recite

O Jatavedas, the inspiration to descend to the world of mortals and the inspiration to survey the state of that world comes from you. The capacity to comprehend the conditions in which mortals live and my inclination to join them also comes from you. Living with humans while simultaneously being with you is a special privilege. This exclusive privilege is the ground for articulating your unconditional love and compassion in these fifteen mantras. Propelled by your will, I exercise my exclusive privilege and proclaim that as long as the seven sages (the Big Dipper) shine in the sky, these fifteen mantras will remain untouched by human frailty. They will serve as the mantric locus of the Divine Mother Sri Lakshmi. Those who aspire to gain inner prosperity and wish it to last forever should recite these mantras with a clear mind and a pure heart. I also proclaim that the inner prosperity invoked by these mantras will awaken prosperity in the external world. The mind of those reciting these mantras will gravitate toward uplifting thoughts. Their speech and action will conform to both the implicit and explicit content of these mantras.

It is my promise that those who practice and assimilate these mantras will be blessed with the company of Sri Lakshmi. As the practice matures in successive stages, these mantras will reveal ever subtler and more potent meanings and powers, impelling practitioners to become increasingly vigilant and diligent. They will know intuitively how to further refine their practice and become a perfect container of love, grace, guidance, and protection. In her own mysterious way, the divine radiance of Jatavedas will walk into the lives of practitioners as guru, guide, and provider.

The Practice of Sri Sukta

The exposition of Sri Sukta offered in the previous chapter shows us that each mantra is a storehouse of unimaginably vast power and wisdom. As we have seen, Sri Sukta is the living body of the sages to whom it was first revealed. A thorough study of these mantras reconfirms the biblical proclamation: "In the beginning was the Word, and the Word was with God, and the Word was God." By reflecting on the inner meaning of these mantras, we come to understand the truth and power of the Vedantic pronouncement: "The knower of Brahman becomes Brahman." The more we contemplate on the meaning of these mantras, the closer we come to the seers of the mantras. The closer we are to the seers who received and embodied the mantras, the greater our access to the wealth these mantras contain. The key to a successful practice of Sri Sukta lies in reading these mantras again and again, reflecting on their meaning, and assimilating them so completely that they become part of our constant awareness.

As stated earlier, the most common application of Sri Sukta is to overcome poverty, which has long been associated with the lack of material resources to meet daily needs. But those who understand the dynamics of inner poverty and its effect on our thought, speech, and action, as well as on the larger world of which we are a part, apply these mantras to acquire a prosperity so highly refined that it drives away all forms of poverty and destitution. Because the goddess Lakshmi is associated with wealth in modern Hindu mythology and because the word *Lakshmi* occurs several times in Sri Sukta, people unfamiliar with Vedic and tantric philosophy believe that Sri Sukta is a prayer to appease the goddess Lakshmi, the consort of the god Vishnu. This view lacks the philosophical and metaphysical refinement necessary to benefit fully from the practice of Sri Sukta.

Sri Sukta is part of the *Rig Veda* and thus was revealed before the advent of Hinduism and Hindu mythology. The concept of Brahma, Vishnu, and Shiva as the three governing gods of the universe does not exist in the *Rig Veda,* and there is only a cursory reference to Lakshmi's association with Vishnu as his consort. The most prominent divinity invoked in the Vedas is Agni, the sacred fire; Sri Lakshmi is the intrinsic shakti of Agni. She is the omniscience of the omniscient being, Agni. Because of this intrinsic omniscience, Agni is called Jatavedas, the omniscient being. Omnipotence and omnipresence are the ever-expanding capacities of Agni's omniscience, Sri Lakshmi. This understanding enables us to transcend our cultural and religious limitations, a prerequisite for optimizing the practice of Sri Sukta.

Before examining the multilevel practices of Sri Sukta, we need to familiarize ourselves with the traditional understanding of these mantras. According to the tradition, although each mantra has a unique power and function, they all share a common mantric shakti. Like all mantras belonging to the tradition of Sri Vidya, the mantras of Sri Sukta originate from the primordial pool of *tritari. Tritari* means "the three who help you cross." In this context, tritari refers to three bija mantras that give us the ability to cross from this shore of life to the next, from the undesirable to the desirable, from that which is binding to freedom. These bija mantras are *aim, hrim,* and *shrim.*

The power inherent in *aim* enables us to distinguish truth from untruth, real from unreal, good from bad, and right from wrong. This bija mantra embodies the power of knowledge. It awakens and illuminates the discerning power of our mind. It frees us from doubt, fills us with confidence, and sets a clear direction.

The power inherent in *hrim,* the second bija mantra of tritari, enables the mind to discover the tools and means for attaining the goal. It draws our hidden wealth to us and transports us to where our wealth is hidden. It creates a condition where we bump into our fortune. In short, the mantric shakti of *hrim* presides over our destiny. Choosing a good destiny and discarding a bad one is the intrinsic capacity of *aim,* which precedes *hrim* in tritari.

The inherent power of *shrim,* the third bija mantra of tritari, infuses the process of inner illumination (the function of *aim*) and inner discovery (the function of *hrim*) with beauty and joy. *Shrim* banishes dryness from our quest. It nullifies tendencies that force us to perceive life as bondage. It infuses our mind with positive thoughts and transforms our worldview. *Shrim* enables us to see life in the world as a wave of beauty and joy, and thus inspires us to find freedom in the world, not from the world.

Starting Out

According to the tradition, the inherent power of tritari—*aim, hrim,* and *shrim*—is the overarching shakti of all the mantras of Sri Sukta. For this reason, adepts in the tradition advise seekers to make Sri Sukta an integral part of any practice. There are a number of ways Sri Sukta can be integrated into daily practice: You can recite it before beginning your main course of meditation or once you have completed it. You can integrate it into your practice or treat it as an independent practice; you can also recite Sri Sukta without linking it to your practice. In order to benefit fully, remember that Sri Sukta has nothing to do with belief or disbelief in a religion or deity. As long as you believe in truth, which existed before you were born and will continue to exist after you have gone, you are a perfect candidate for practicing Sri Sukta. As long as you believe that the unknown facets of life outnumber the known, you are qualified to practice it. And as long as this understanding makes you humble enough to seek love, guidance, protection, and nourishment from the inner dimensions of truth, your practice of Sri Sukta will exert its magic on your mind and heart. The forces governing your inner and outer worlds will conform to the shakti incessantly flowing from Sri Sukta.

If memorizing all the mantras seems too difficult, select one mantra and use it as a prayer at the beginning of your practice. If that prayer constitutes your entire practice, recite the mantra you have selected eleven times every day.

To decide which of these mantras to choose, read the exposition in the prior chapter and see what resonates with your heart. Here is some guidance:

- If you suffer from feelings of unworthiness, or if you gravitate toward self-denigrating thoughts, feelings, and behaviors, choose the first mantra. The leading force of this mantra is *Hiranyavarna*, the resplendent pulsation of the life force. It will help you banish self-denigrating thoughts and prevent you from gravitating toward low-grade actions.

- If you struggle with cyclical failures in worldly or spiritual pursuits and wish to have a stable and successful life, choose the second mantra.
- If your struggles are due to discord and conflict with your loved ones, friends, and family, adopt the fourth mantra.
- If stinginess is your main problem, practice the fifth mantra.
- If you strive for prosperity, recognition, and prominence, and at the same time suffer from possessiveness and an inability to let go, and this seems to be the cause of your inner unrest, choose the seventh mantra.
- If you feel you are aging faster mentally than physically and your mind is being sucked into a sense of emptiness, practice the eighth mantra.
- If you feel you are being oppressed and it seems that dark and destructive forces are trying to govern your life, and if you feel you are not able to get the freedom and justice you deserve, and further, that these conditions are destroying your health and peace of mind, then you should practice the ninth mantra.
- If you notice your body and mind are unable to extract and assimilate nourishment from food and rejuvenating thoughts and practices, or if you notice you are unable to get rid of physical, mental, or spiritual waste matter, the ninth mantra will be best for you.
- If your joy comes from serving the natural world and you feel gratified when you see that the soil, water, and air are healthy, practice the thirteenth mantra.
- If your happiness and contentment come from being surrounded by high-minded, loving, trustworthy kinsmen and friends, as well as from being part of a balanced web of life, choose the fifteenth mantra.

Begin your practice in whatever manner feels comfortable, but remember, Sri Sukta is the sages' gift to humankind. Its mantric power is immense. It holds the solution to our most fundamental problem: how to overcome conditions that threaten our survival, progress, freedom, and fulfillment, and how to acquire the tools and means to ensure our physical, mental, and spiritual well-being. Sri Sukta has the power to uproot this fundamental problem. Working with mantras of this stature is a privilege and must not be taken lightly. Sri Sukta is much more than a set of prayers and is not a verbal ornament for ceremonial events.

Formal Practice: Stage One

The practice of Sri Sukta is traditionally done in three successive stages. Memorizing all sixteen mantras is the first requirement. If this is too difficult, begin by memorizing only the ninth mantra. Once you have memorized it, recite it 3 times for the first 3 days and 11 times for the next 11 days. For the next 108 days, recite the ninth mantra 108 times each day. Your mala has 108 beads and can be used to track your recitations. If 108 recitations take too much time, then do the recitations in two sittings of 54 each. Meanwhile, continue memorizing the remaining fifteen mantras. In addition to many other applications, yogis in our tradition have long used the ninth mantra to sharpen the power of memory. In four months you will have the entire Sri Sukta memorized and will have gained speed in reciting it. Thereafter begins the formal practice of stage one.

The first stage consists of reciting Sri Sukta 800 times in no more than 80 days and not less than 40. If you do 10 recitations a day, you will complete the 800 recitations in 80 days; if you do

20 recitations a day, you will complete the recitations in 40 days. A time-and-number-bound practice such as this is known as a *purashcharana*. Once you have begun, you must not increase or decrease the number of daily recitations, so before you begin this purashcharana, do 3 recitations of Sri Sukta daily, in one sitting, for a few weeks or months. During the first and second recitations, omit the sixteenth mantra; recite it only at the end of the third and final recitation. These 3 daily recitations are not part of the purashcharana. Do it for your pleasure and to help you assess how much time it will take to complete 10 or 20 recitations. If you have practiced and have gained proficiency, 10 recitations will not take more than thirty minutes. Do your daily recitations in one sitting, if possible, but in not more than two. Remember, in each sitting, the sixteenth mantra is recited only during the final recitation.

During the course of the practice, avoid eating stale food. Avoid situations where you lose your temper or speak foul words. Do not involve yourself in actions that lead to feelings of remorse. Do not do this practice with the intention of achieving a worldly goal. During the course of the practice, if the desire for worldly success enters your mind, surrender it to the Divine Being as soon as you become aware of it. But do not—under any circumstance—identify yourself as a poor practitioner should such a thought enter your mind.

After you have completed the practice, take another 8 or 4 days (depending on the length of your practice) to make fire offerings with one-tenth of the number of recitations you did as part of your daily practice. Thus, if you completed the practice in 80 days, add 8 days for a fire offering. If you completed the practice in 40 days, add 4 days for a fire offering. In both cases, do 10 recitations each day, making a fire offering with each of the first fifteen mantras. The offering with the sixteenth mantra is the concluding offering of each daily session.

Throughout these 88 or 44 days, it is important that you read the commentary on at least a few of the mantras each day and reflect on their meaning. This will help you find and maintain your connection with the shakti these mantras embody.

The standard ingredients for the fire offerings include sesame seeds, sugar, and ghee. You can dig a fire pit in the ground or use a portable fire pit. Make sure you are familiar with the basic mantras for purifying the space around the fire pit and igniting the fire.

Yogis in our tradition bypass external fire rituals, however. They identify their own body as a living abode of sacred fire. During the first stage of Sri Sukta sadhana, they invoke the sacred fire at their navel center. This is where they arrange their karmic firewood and light it with the flame of knowledge (*jnana*) and nonattachment (*vairagya*). The ingredients of their offerings are trustful surrender combined with love and conviction. While maintaining awareness of this internal sacred fire at the navel center, they recite Sri Sukta, adding *svaha* at the end of each mantra and making an internal offering.

The successful practice of this time-and-number-bound purashcharana of Sri Sukta is a necessary step for imbibing the essence of Sri Sukta, as well as for establishing an everlasting bond with the sages to whom it was revealed. Thereafter, you can use the entire Sri Sukta or a particular mantra for either spiritual or material benefits.

Formal Practice: Stage Two

The second stage of Sri Sukta is more intense and potent than the first stage. As in the first stage, the course of the practice consists of 800 recitations. However, this time the practice is completed in 11 days, plus an extra day for the fire offering, so the entire practice takes 12 days. There are strict rules about when and how to do the practice. It must begin the day after the new moon—begin in the early morning of the first day of the bright fortnight. The fire offering must take place on the 12th day of the bright fortnight and must be completed before the 12th day ends.

Unlike in the first stage, making an offering into the sacred fire is not optional. Therefore, preparation for this stage of the practice requires learning the fundamentals of tantric rituals. These include the dynamics of sacred fire, the spiritual counterpart of the physical fire, and the mantras for invoking and lighting the fire. These fundamentals also include a basic understanding of the techniques employed in rituals—the sequence in which different aspects of rituals are arranged, the spiritual properties of the ingredients of the offering, and the tantric principles used in determining the ratio of these different ingredients.

The most important requirement is the formal initiation into the tradition of Sri Vidya. This initiation can be done only by a competent teacher—someone who has been formally initiated by an adept and has undergone rigorous practice. Such a teacher has been taught the subtle details of the lineage—the precise nature of the *ishta deva* (the identifiable attributes of nameless and formless divinity), the relationship between the ishta deva and the *rishi* (seer), the precise mantra of the ishta deva, and how the human body serves as a seat for the ishta deva. A teacher of this caliber makes an intuitive assessment of the student's strengths and weaknesses. On the basis of this assessment, the teacher decides how to bridge the gap between the first and second stages of the practice and confers initiation into the shakti mantra most appropriate for that student. The practice of the shakti mantra builds the foundation for undertaking the second stage of Sri Sukta sadhana. For example, the practice of *gayatri* mantra, *maha mrityunjaya* mantra, or *navarna* mantra is prescribed in most cases for building this foundation.

Observances accompanying the second stage of the practice are stricter than in the first stage. The most important of these observances is *shaucha,* cleanliness. Cleanliness is twofold: external and internal. External cleanliness involves keeping your home and surroundings clean. For example, not only must you keep your meditation room clean, but the rest of your dwelling as well. The space outside your door should be clean. Your shoes should be clean and arranged properly, and your clothes should be clean, folded, and put in the right place. Dirty dishes compromise the sanctity of your home. Before you go to bed, all your household objects should be put in their right place. Make your bed as soon as you get up. The goal is to maintain an environment in which your senses of sight, smell, taste, touch, and hearing do not contact anything dirty, disorganized, undesirable, unpleasant, or unhealthy.

Internal cleanliness is equally important. This includes keeping not only your body and garments clean, but also your internal organs and mind. A few days before beginning this practice, detoxify your body. Apply the yogic and ayurvedic methods of cleansing your gastrointestinal tract. Fasting, juicing, sweating, and deep relaxation are all detoxifying. During this 12-day practice, follow a strict diet. Eat only food that is freshly cooked, light, and nutritious. Maintain a lifestyle that ensures you will not suffer from indigestion or constipation.

Mental cleanliness requires that you refrain from entertaining negative thoughts. Of all negative tendencies, jealousy, anger, fear, and greed are the most detrimental to this practice. These tendencies are subtle and do not go away just because shortly before you began your practice you made a decision not to entertain them, so it is important to examine your habitual tendencies far in advance. Try your best to eradicate these deep-rooted tendencies. Cultivate an attitude of friendliness toward those who appear to be happier and more successful than you are, compassion for those who are suffering, happiness toward those who exhibit virtuous qualities, and a nonjudgmental attitude toward those who appear to be wrongdoers. Identify your most stubborn negative tendency as well as the circumstances that trigger it—observe how this tendency asserts itself powerfully and without warning. Consciously cultivate a habit of practicing contemplation on that which is diametrically opposed to your most stubborn negative tendency. The great master Patanjali calls this contemplative process *pratipaksha-bhavana*. In other words, adopt a yogic worldview and meditative practice to cultivate a mind that is clear, peaceful, free from fear, and has the ability to maintain constant awareness of higher reality. Such a highly trained mind eventually loses the taste for harboring negative tendencies, a condition necessary to practice the second stage of Sri Sukta with precision and perfection.

The selection of a place for undertaking this practice is as important as the time. Choose a quiet place surrounded by the beauty of nature. A riverbank, especially the bank of a river that flows to the sea (*samudra-gamini*)—such as the Ganga, the Nile, and the Mississippi—is highly suitable. So is a spiritually vibrant place, especially a fully consecrated shrine. Even at a shrine or on a riverbank, the cleanliness of the place and the aesthetics of the surrounding area should be befitting the standards of the queen of beauty and joy invoked by Sri Sukta.

It is important that during this practice you are accompanied by select friends who understand what you are doing and have respect for it. During this intense practice, these loved ones ensure you have everything you need and ward off external disturbances before they come to your attention.

This stage of Sri Sukta sadhana is accompanied by ancillary practices. Some of these practices are for purification of the surroundings as well as purification of your mental landscape. Others are for invoking the benevolent forces of nature, the presiding divinities of the mantras, the sages of the tradition, and most importantly, the shaktis that reside in Sri Chakra. The final step of these ancillary practices is the invocation of the shaktis presiding over the mantras of Sri Sukta. You can have Sri Chakra inscribed on a gold plate or on quartz as a locus for these shaktis. A vessel filled with water is equally appropriate. When all of this is in place, begin the recitation of Sri Sukta.

During these 12 days, start your practice only after you have bathed and put on clean clothes. Please remember: both inner and outer cleanliness is an integral part of this practice. According to the rules laid down in the scriptures, you begin the recitation only after having completed your daily minimum course of the shakti mantra into which you were initiated. The rules dictate that you do 73 recitations daily for the first 8 days and 72 recitations daily for the next 3 days. This brings the total to 800 recitations in 11 days.

If you are extremely disciplined and well practiced, you will be able to do the entire course of daily recitations in one sitting. However, do not force yourself to do this. If you need to take a break, do so only after completing the entire Sri Sukta, including the sixteenth mantra. Return to your seat only after you have washed your hands and feet and rinsed your mouth. Before you resume your recitation, do one mala of the shakti mantra into which you were initiated. Your final segment of recitation should end with the sixteenth mantra of Sri Sukta.

The 12th day begins with a fire offering. In this second stage, the fire offering is more elaborate than in the previous stage. These offerings are made into a properly consecrated *havan kunda* (sacred fireplace). The tantric method of consecration is known as *prana pratishtha*. *Prana pratishtha* means "invoking and establishing prana, the life force." If you do not have access to a preconsecrated fireplace, then request a qualified practitioner to do a temporary prana pratishtha for you in advance of your Sri Sukta fire offering. This can be done a month, a week, or even a few days before you need to conclude your practice with the fire offering. After this temporary prana pratishtha, the sanctity of the fireplace is to be maintained until you have completed the fire offering. Because you are fully engaged in the practice of Sri Sukta itself, this is to be done by someone else.

The procedure of the fire offering includes the invocation of thirty-three categories of divinities known as *Vishve Deva*, followed by the invocation of Ganesha, the divinity that presides over the forces that remove obstacles and bring stability; the *Dikpalas*, the protectors of directions; and the *Grahas*, the presiding forces of the planets. Then ignite the fire in the fireplace with the appropriate mantras. After igniting the fire, the first 9 offerings are made to Jatavedas Agni. These offerings are accompanied by the first nine mantras of the *Rig Veda*. Then make 108 offerings with the shakti mantra into which you were initiated. Thereafter, begin making offerings with the fifteen mantras of Sri Sukta and continue until you have completed 80 recitations. Recite the sixteenth mantra only at the end of the 80th recitation. This is the shortest procedure. If you find even this short procedure too elaborate, seek help from someone who is proficient in this science.

It is important to plan your fire offering properly. Keep enough firewood and offering ingredients within easy reach. Someone sensible and sensitive to what you are doing should always be nearby in case of an emergency. If you need to take a break, do it only after completing the entire Sri Sukta, ending with the sixteenth mantra. Make the break as brief as possible. Maintain an uninterrupted awareness and refrain from distractions. Before taking your seat, wash your hands and feet and rinse your mouth. Resume your fire offering with 108 offerings accompanied by the shakti mantra; then immediately return to Sri Sukta. The final round ends with the sixteenth mantra followed by 108 offerings with the shakti mantra.

Once you have finished, you must not collect the offering ingredients that may have fallen outside the fireplace nor put them into the sacred fire. You may remove the utensils, the unused firewood, and the offering ingredients, but do it carefully, without slighting the still-burning fire. Do not disturb the fire or the fireplace until the ash is completely cold. The fireplace and the area surrounding it are still occupied by the divinities that were invoked. Therefore, make sure neither you nor anyone else disturbs the sanctity of the place. Once the ash has cooled, it can be scattered in nature.

Stage two of Sri Sukta sadhana gives your mind an opportunity to fully connect with and assimilate the mantric essence of Sri Sukta. The mantras of Sri Sukta are awakened and remain awakened throughout your life and beyond. This degree of awakening transports you to a state where there is no need to make a formal request to Sri Lakshmi to help, guide, protect, and nurture you. You know she is always with you, in you, and all around you. This trust outweighs all the world's gifts combined. This practice fills you with the conviction that your prayers and requests can never be denied. This conviction further brightens your power of discernment; thus your conscience will not permit you to pray for petty things. Thereafter, your joy comes from knowing you have become a worthy conduit for transmitting the gifts of Divine Mother Sri Lakshmi to the world. Your intentions will bear fruit. After completing this second stage, any goal-driven practice of Sri Sukta undertaken by you will yield unfailing results.

Because these mantras are now mature and residing in your mind in their fully awakened state, the tradition urges you to articulate them to others judiciously. In the words of the scriptures: "Mantra Vidya approached the adept and spoke: 'Promise you will protect me from falling into the hands of those who are unworthy. Only when I am protected and nourished will I be able to protect and nourish you.'" In other words, the second stage of the practice gives you the ability to transmit this knowledge to others. And this capacity of transmission comes with a high degree of responsibility. Honoring that responsibility is the most appropriate love offering you can make to the tradition, which holds preserving this knowledge as its highest duty.

Formal Practice: Stage Three

From the standpoint of practice, the third stage of Sri Sukta sadhana is almost forbidden. It consists of extremely technical and tightly guarded practices, which are undertaken either by adepts in complete seclusion or by highly motivated aspirants working under the direct supervision of one or more adepts. This stage of the practice is rarely done for personal benefit.

To give you a sense of the expansive nature of the practice at this stage, I will provide a succinct description of Maha Pushti Yaga, a rare practice for invoking the forces of nourishment to nullify fourteen distinct conditions that drain the sap of life. This unique practice is mentioned in *Netra Tantra*; it is elaborated somewhat in *Sri Vidyarnava*, but the details necessary to do the practice are available only through the living tradition. The practice of Maha Pushti Yaga builds on the practice of Rudra Yaga, described in scriptures like *Netra Tantra*, and the practice of Sri Chakra, described in scriptures like *Parashurama Kalpa Sutra*. There is no written record that explains how to connect these two practices. That is the job of the tradition. Furthermore, there is no written record of how to erect the spiritual structure of Maha Pushti Yaga on the firm foundation of the perfectly blended practice of Rudra Yaga and Sri Chakra.

In Maha Pushti Yaga, the ninth mantra of Sri Sukta takes the leading role—a secret passed on only to those who have both completed the second stage of Sri Sukta sadhana and the practice of Rudra Yaga with the *maha mrityunjaya* mantra, as well as the practice of Sri Chakra with one of the Sri Vidya mantras. This practice is done with the precise intention of accelerating the process of nourishment and nullifying fourteen conditions that drain the sap of life. Those conditions are:

1. *Bhuta,* literally, "past, ghost, dead." It is a state where the present is haunted by useless memories of the past. Practically speaking, it is a state of mind unable to let go of the past. It is marked by *shunya,* emptiness, loneliness, and purposelessness. It is crowded with the contents of the past, grief, feelings of regret, and the desire for revenge. It is also marked by *kupa,* a condition that turns the body and mind into a landfill. This condition grows into an inability to get rid of unwanted waste matter—physical, mental, and spiritual. The inability to let go of the past manifests in *eka-vriksha,* a con-

dition which makes us feel we are like a lonely tree, with no association and interaction with others. We do not feel like sharing our sorrow and joy with others. Another aspect of this debilitating condition is *chattvara,* literally, "crossings." It refers to being caught in the crosscurrents of past conditioning, which cripples our ability to make a decision about the future course of life.

2. *Yaksha,* an unmanageably distorted power of mind leading to hallucinations; the strongest trait of one's personality; uncontrolled behavior; cynicism
3. *Graha,* strong attachment; a habit of worry so strong that the person unconsciously looks for reasons to worry
4. *Unmada,* insanity; powerful impulse of *kama* (desire) and *kroda* (anger) that is so deep and intense and flows from inside so unconsciously that the person has no control over his speech and action
5. *Shakini,* tendencies that force human beings to embrace hypocrisy; the force behind double standards; the unconscious impulse to wear more than one mask; deceitful tendencies to hurt and harm others for one's selfish motives
6. *Yogini,* presiding forces of chakras in the human body that have gone haywire
7. *Bhagini,* distorted and imbalanced energy field of the body and senses
8. *Rudra mata,* distorted and imbalanced prana, the life force
9. *Davi,* distorted and imbalanced power of the intellect and discernment
10. *Damari,* distorted and imbalanced field and function of the force of revelation
11. *Rupita,* deep-rooted tendency for mental, verbal, and physical violence

12. *Apasmara,* an uncontrolled mental outburst so intense that the response of the brain and nervous system far exceeds one's physical capacity
13. *Pishacha,* suicidal tendencies
14. *Brahma-raksho-graha,* powerful impressions created by acting against one's conscience so powerfully one fails to forgive oneself and remains remorseful

Another example of practice at this stage is Maha Shanti Yaga, which is for invoking eighteen categories of peace. This practice is mentioned in two scriptures: *Durga Saptashati* and *Sri Vidyarnava.* The tradition preserves the knowledge regarding how to elaborate the practice mentioned in these two scriptures, how to connect Rudra Yaga with Sri Chakra, how to invoke the 360 shaktis of *Durga Saptashati* in the Sri Chakra, and then how to invoke Sri Sukta and request the mantric shaktis of Sri Sukta to preside over the Maha Shanti Yaga. The following description of the eighteen categories of peace will give you an idea of how profound and structured the practice is at this stage and why a practice of this caliber is forbidden.

1. *Vaishnavi*, an atmosphere marked by stability, nourishment, safety, security, and protection
2. *Aindri*, an atmosphere of obedience to nature's laws
3. *Brahmi*, an atmosphere guided by a highly evolved intelligence and ideology
4. *Raudri*, an atmosphere free of anger, fear, and violence
5. *Vayavya*, an atmosphere nourished by the peaceful functions of the wind
6. *Varuni*, an atmosphere nourished by the peaceful functions of water

7. *Kauberi*, an atmosphere conducive to the creation and circulation of wealth
8. *Bhargavi*, an atmosphere in which prosperity, beauty, and entertainment are balanced
9. *Prajapatya*, an atmosphere where the bond between progeny and the progeniture, children and parents, is pure, strong, and unending
10. *Tvastri*, an atmosphere that is conducive to construction and manufacturing
11. *Kaumari*, an atmosphere conducive to innocence, purity, and simplicity
12. *Agneyi*, an atmosphere nourished by the peaceful functions of fire
13. *Marudgana*, an atmosphere free from forty-nine different forms of storms
14. *Gandharvi*, an atmosphere conducive to the fine arts and creative expression
15. *Nairitaki*, an atmosphere free of poverty and disease
16. *Angirasi*, an atmosphere conducive to spiritual practices and fulfillment
17. *Yamya*, an atmosphere free of fear of death
18. *Parthavi*, an atmosphere free from earthly disruptions and chaos

History is rife with evidence of the human tendency to exploit and misuse knowledge, technology, and scientific discoveries. Fear, greed, and the desire for distinction are the major causes of this widespread exploitation and misuse. In regard to science and technology, which normally focuses on making us smarter and more successful in the material world, we establish rules and regulations, although these are violated more often than honored.

The result is many scientific discoveries that could have helped humanity have instead caused untold harm.

Tantric knowledge and achievements are no exception. Scriptures have documented the consequences of misusing these practices. Knowing that this behavior is almost impossible to eradicate, adepts skillfully hid this knowledge and imposed a long, complex series of barriers to accessing it. They made sure that the rules for practicing this science are even stricter than the disciplines necessary to gain intellectual knowledge of it.

The tantric masters recognized that the more subtle and potent the knowledge, the more important it is to impose strict, subtle, and highly potent rules and strictures for accessing and using that knowledge. No rules and strictures are more effective and potent than the requirement to purify our mind and cultivate a willingness to hear and heed the call of our conscience. For this reason, these enlightened adepts created a system whereby we must go through a long and strenuous process of inner purification and self-discovery. The result is that by the time we reach the threshold of this knowledge, we have become keenly aware of what is truly good, as opposed to what is merely attractive and exciting. That is why the most important requirement for practicing this third stage of Sri Sukta is understanding the value of the injunctions imposed at this stage and finding joy in honoring them. Working toward gaining this understanding is a practice in itself, for this understanding opens the door to the inner dynamics of Sri Sukta.

Sri Sukta is one of the greatest gifts of the ancient sages. It holds the key to our inner peace, prosperity, and well-being. It holds the key to creating a new reality, a reality in which we can conceive and nurture a collective consciousness healthy enough and rich enough to build an enlightened society. It holds the key to finding our connection with nature and nature's forces, thus opening the floodgates of a prosperity that transcends all geographical and cultural boundaries. Sri Sukta is a link between us—the mortal beings—and the immortal ones, whose happiness comes from seeing us happy.

APPENDICES

APPENDIX A

Sri Sukta

(from the Rig Veda, Khailakani Suktani)

MANTRA 1

हिरण्यवर्णां हरिणीं सुवर्णरजतस्रजाम् ।
चन्द्रां हिरण्मयीं लक्ष्मीं जातवेदो म आवह ॥१॥

hiraṇyavarṇām hariṇīm suvarṇarajatasrajām
candrām hiraṇmayīm lakṣmīm jātavedo ma āvaha ||1||

O Jatavedas, please carry me to or bring to me the Divine Mother Lakshmi, the supreme beauty, the goddess as resplendent as gold, garlanded with gold and silver, delightful as the moon—the essence of gold embodying all forms of prosperity.

hiraṇyavarṇām, the one who is as pure and resplendent as gold

hariṇīm, the beautiful, blossoming; the female deer (at one time, Lakshmi turned herself into a doe); the one who resides in Hari, Vishnu, or the one in whom Hari resides

suvarṇarajatasrajām, the one who is garlanded with gold and silver; the one who wears the garland of flowers made of, or as resplendent as, gold and silver

candrām, the moon; the one who is as cooling and soothing as moonlight

hiraṇmayīm, the one who is the embodiment of gold; the one who is molten gold—living prosperity

lakṣmīm, the goddess of prosperity; the divinity endowed with all auspiciousness and goodness

jātavedas, O Omniscient Fire; O Most Sacred Fire presiding over rituals

ma, to me

āvaha, bring her from every direction in every respect

MANTRA 2

तां म आवह जातवेदो लक्ष्मीमनपगामिनीम् ।
यस्यां हिरण्यं विन्देयं गामश्वं पुरुषानहम् ॥ २ ॥

tām ma āvaha jātavedo lakṣmīmanapagāminīm
yasyām hiraṇyam vindeyam gāmaśvam puruṣānaham
||2||

O Jatavedas, please carry me to or bring to me the Divine Mother Lakshmi, the one who once having come never goes away. In her may I obtain gold, cows, horses, and manpower.

tām, to her
ma, to me
āvaha, bring her from every direction in every respect
jātavedas, O Omniscient Fire; O Most Sacred Fire presiding over rituals
lakṣmīm, the goddess of prosperity; the divinity endowed with all auspiciousness and goodness
anapagāminīm, the one who does not go away
yasyām, in the one in whom
hiraṇyam, gold
vindeyam, derived from the verb *vid*, to obtain; may I obtain
gām, cows
aśvam, horses
puruṣān, humans; manpower
aham, I

MANTRA 3

अश्वपूर्वां रथमध्यां हस्तिनादप्रबोधिनीम् ।
श्रियं देवीं उपह्वये श्रीर्मा देवी जुषताम् ॥३॥

aśvapūrvām rathamadhyām hastinādaprabodhinīm
śriyam devīm upahvaye śrīrmā devī juṣatām ||3||

I invoke Sri [the Divine Mother Sri Vidya], along with her retinue, with horses in the front and a chariot in the center; her arrival is announced by *nada*, the trumpeting of elephants. May Devi, the shining being, engage me in her service as she pleases.

aśvapūrvām, the one who has horses in front
rathamadhyām, the one who has a chariot in the middle
hastinādaprabodhinīm, the one who awakens [us] with the trumpeting of elephants
śriyam, the Divine Mother Sri Vidya; the goddess of beauty and bliss
devīm, the Devi; the shining being
upahvaye, I invoke
śrīḥ, the Divine Mother Sri Vidya
ma, to me
devī, the shining being
juṣatām, be pleased

MANTRA 4

कां सोस्मितां हिरण्यप्राकारां आर्द्रां ज्वलन्तीं तृप्तां तर्पयन्तीम् ।
पद्मे स्थितां पद्मवर्णां तामिहोपह्वये श्रियम् ॥४॥

kām sosmitām hiraṇyaprākārām ārdrām
jvalantīm tṛptām tarpayantīm
padme sthitām padmavarṇām tāmihopahvaye śriyam ||4||

I invoke Sri [the Divine Mother Sri Vidya], who is the creative intelligence of the creator, whose countenance has a slight smile, who is surrounded by a wall of gold; the one who is moist, the one who is lustrous, the one who is content, the one who confers contentment, the one who is seated on the lotus, the one who is identical to the lotus.

kām, the creative intelligence of the creator
sosmitām, with a hint of a smile
hiraṇyaprākārām, the one who is surrounded by a wall of gold
ārdrām, the moist one
jvalantīm, the radiant being
tṛptām, the one who is content
tarpayantīm, the one who grants contentment
padme sthitām, the one who sits on the lotus
padmavarṇām, the one who is identical to the lotus
tām, to that [Sri]
iha, here
upahvaye, I invoke
śriyam, the Divine Mother Sri Vidya; the goddess of beauty and bliss

MANTRA 5

चन्द्रां प्रभासां यशसा ज्वलन्तीं श्रियं लोके
देवजुष्टामुदाराम् ।
ताम् पद्मिनीमीं शरणं प्रपद्ये अलक्ष्मीर् मे नश्यतां त्वां
वृणोमि ॥५॥

candrām prabhāsām yaśasā jvalantīm śriyam loke
devajuṣṭāmudārām
tām padminīm īm śaraṇam prapadye alakṣmīr me
naśyatām tvām vṛṇomi ||5||

I take refuge in Sri, who is delightful, uniquely lit, shining with glory, revered and attended by luminous beings, and

known in the world through her generosity. I take refuge in that Sri who embodies the lotus and who as the sound *īm* forms the core of the seed mantra of Sri Lakshmi. May my inner and outer poverty be destroyed.

candrām, the one who is as delightful as the moon
prabhāsām, the resplendent one
yaśasā, with glory
jvalantīm, the glowing one
śriyam, the Divine Mother Sri Vidya
loke, in the world
devajuṣṭām, revered and attended by luminous beings
udārām, the one who is generous
tām, to that [Sri]
padminīm, the one who embodies the lotus, sits on the lotus, or wears lotus garlands
īm, shakti mantra forming the core of *hrīm*, the *bija* mantra of Sri Lakshmi
śaraṇam, refuge; shelter
prapadye, I surrender
alakṣmīḥ, lack of prosperity; lack of wealth; lack of beauty and goodness
me, my
naśyatām, be destroyed
tvām, you (to you)
vṛṇomi, I embrace; I choose

MANTRA 6

आदित्यवर्णे तपसोऽधिजातो वनस्पतिस्तव वृक्षोऽथ बिल्वः ।
तस्य फलानि तपसानुदन्तु यान्तरा याश्च बाह्या अलक्ष्मीः ॥६॥

ādityavarṇe tapaso'dhijāto vanaspatistava vṛkṣo'tha bilvaḥ
tasya phalāni tapasānudantu yāntarā yāśca bāhyā alakṣmīḥ ||6||

O Sun-bright Divinity, the Bilva tree, the lord of the forest, is born from your *tapas*. Through *tapas* one attains the fruits of that tree. Please drive away all my internal and external destitution.

ādityavarṇe, O Sun-bright Divinity
tapasaḥ, from tapas
adhijataḥ, that has been born
vanaspatis, the lord of the forest
tava, your
vṛkṣaḥ, tree
atha, a word denoting auspiciousness
bilvaḥ, Bilva tree (*Aegle marmelos*)
tasya, of that
phalāni, fruits
tapasā, with tapas; through tapas
nudantu, to remove

yā, that which
antarā, internal
yāśca, and that which
bāhyā, external
alakṣmīḥ, lack of prosperity; lack of goodness and beauty

MANTRA 7

उपैतु मां देवसखः कीर्तिश्च मणिना सह ।
प्रादुर्भूतोऽस्मि राष्ट्रेऽस्मिन् कीर्तिमृद्धिं ददातु मे ॥७॥

upaitu mām devasakhaḥ kīrtiśca maṇinā saha
prādurbhūto'smi rāṣṭre'smin kīrtimṛddhim
dadātu me ||7||

May the friend of deva, the bright being accompanied by Kirti and Mani, come to me. I am born in this land. Please bless me with glory and wealth.

upaitu, please come
mām, to me
devasakhaḥ, friend of deva, the bright being; friend of Rudra, embodiment of the life force
kīrtiḥ, glory; the quality that makes one glorious; the power that accompanies glory
ca, and
maṇinā, with Mani, more precisely Chintamani, the wish-fulfilling gem; or with Manibhadra, the divine being who gives access to the celestial wealth

saha, with
prādurbhūtaḥ, have been born
asmi, I am
rāṣṭre, in a country; belonging to a country
asmin, in this
kīrtim, glory
ṛddhim, wealth
dadātu me, give me

MANTRA 8

क्षुत्पिपासामलां ज्येष्ठामलक्ष्मीं नाशयाम्यहम् ।
अभूतिमसमृद्धिञ्च सर्वां निर्णुद मे गृहात् ॥८॥

kṣutpipāsāmalām jyeṣṭhāmalakṣmīm nāśayāmyaham
abhūtimasamṛddhiñca sarvām nirṇuda me gṛhāt ||8||

I eliminate hunger, thirst, impurity, decrepitude, and poverty. Please remove all forms of emptiness and poverty from my home.

kṣut, hunger
pipāsā, thirst
malām, impurity; toxin; uncleanliness
jyeṣṭhām, the phenomenon of decrepitude; the one who was born before Lakshmi
alakṣmīm, lack of prosperity; lack of goodness and beauty

nāśayāmi, I destroy
aham, I
abhūtim, lack of fullness
asamṛddhiñ, lack of prosperity
ca, and
sarvām, all
nirṇuda, remove
me, my
gṛhāt, from home

MANTRA 9

गन्धद्वारां दुराधर्षां नित्यपुष्टां करीषिणीम् ।
ईश्वरीं सर्वभूतानां तामिहोपह्वये श्रियम् ॥९॥

gandhadvārām durādharṣām nityapuṣṭām karīṣiṇīm
īśvarīm sarvabhūtānām tāmihopahvaye śriyam ||9||

I invoke the Divine Mother Sri, who is the gateway to inner fragrance, who is invincible and eternally nurturing. I invoke the Divine Mother Sri, who embodies the power of will and the power of action, the one who is lord of all living beings.

gandhadvārām, the gateway to fragrance
durādharṣām, unstoppable; invincible
nityapuṣṭām, eternally nurturing; the source of eternal nourishment

karīṣiṇīm, embodiment of the power of will and action; the force that propels the entire process of consuming food—all the way to eliminating waste
īśvarīm, the power of omniscience; the intrinsic omniscience of the omniscient being; might of the almighty
sarva, all
bhūtānām, of living beings
tām, to that [Sri]
iha, here
upahvaye, I invoke
śriyam, the Divine Mother Sri Vidya; the goddess of beauty and bliss

MANTRA 10

मनसः काममाकूतिं वाचः सत्यमशीमहि ।
पशूनां रूपमन्नस्य मयि श्रीः श्रयतां यशः ॥१०॥

manasaḥ kāmamākūtim vācaḥ satyamaśīmahi
paśūnām rūpamannasya mayi śrīḥ śrayatām yaśaḥ ||10||

May I achieve the objects of my desire. May my intentions materialize. May my speech be truthful. May I acquire the full range of cattle and grain. May the Divine Mother Sri and the glory that accompanies her find a home in me.

manasaḥ, of mind; related to the mind
kāmam, desire

ākūtim, intention
vācaḥ, speech
satyam, truth
aśīmahi, may I achieve
paśūnām, of cattle; pertaining to cattle
rūpam, form; essence
annasya, of grain
mayi, in me
śrīḥ, Sri; the Divine Mother; the goddess
śrayatām, may it reside
yaśaḥ, glory; fame

MANTRA 11

कर्दमेन प्रजा भूता मयि संभव कर्दम ।
श्रियं वासय मे कुले मातरं पद्ममालिनीम् ॥ ११ ॥

kardamena prajā bhūtā mayi sambhava kardama
śriyam vāsaya me kule mātaram padmamālinīm ||11||

O Sri, with the birth of Sage Kardama you became a mother. O Kardama, you live in me. Also, please invite Mother Sri, wearing a garland of lotuses, to live in my family.

kardamena, through Sage Kardama; because of Sage Kardama
prajā, unique birth-giver
bhūtā, living beings
mayi, in me

sambhava, be born
kardama, O Sage Kardama
śriyam, the Divine Mother Sri Vidya; the goddess of beauty and bliss
vāsaya, making to dwell
me, my
kule, in the family; in the lineage
mātaram, mother
padmamālinīm, the one who is the embodiment of, or garlanded with, lotuses

MANTRA 12

आपः सृजन्तु स्निग्धानि चिक्लीत वस मे गृहे ।
नि च देवीं मातरं श्रियं वासय मे कुले ॥१२॥

āpaḥ sṛjantu snigdhāni ciklīta vasa me gṛhe
ni ca devīm mātaram śriyam vāsaya me kule ||12||

O Presiding Deity of the Waters, create an atmosphere of love and affection. O Chiklita, son of Divine Mother Sri, please dwell in my home. Furthermore, please invite the Divine Mother Sri to dwell in my family and lineage.

āpaḥ, waters
sṛjantu, please create
snigdhāni, loving; affectionate

ciklīta, a sage
vasa, live
me, my
gṛhe, in the house
ni, completely; fully
ca, and
devīm, the devi; the shining being
mātaram, mother
śriyam, the Divine Mother Sri Vidya; the goddess of beauty and bliss
vāsaya, making to dwell
me, my
kule, in the family; in the lineage

MANTRA 13

आर्द्रां पुष्करिणीं पुष्टिं पिङ्गलां पद्ममालिनीम् ।
चन्द्रां हिरण्मयीं लक्ष्मीं जातवेदो म आवह ॥१३॥

ārdrām puṣkariṇīm puṣṭim piṅgalām padmamālinīm
candrām hiraṇmayīm lakṣmīm jātavedo ma āvaha
||13||

O Jatavedas, please carry me to or bring to me the Divine Mother Lakshmi, who is wet, who presides over lakes and ponds, who is the source of nourishment, who embodies the color of newness, who wears a garland of lotuses, who is as delightful as the moon, and who is as radiant as gold.

ārdrām, wet
puṣkariṇīm, lakes and ponds
puṣṭim, nourishment; source of nourishment
piṅgalām, pinkish color, the color of newness
padmamālinīm, the one who wears the garland of lotuses
candrām, the one who embodies the shakti of the moon
hiraṇmayīm, the one who is the embodiment of gold; the one who is bright like molten gold
lakṣmīm, the goddess of prosperity; the divinity endowed with all auspiciousness and goodness
jātavedas, O Omniscient Fire; O Most Sacred Fire presiding over rituals
ma, to me
āvaha, bring her from every direction in every respect

MANTRA 14

आर्द्रां यः करिणीं यष्टिं सुवर्णां हेममालिनीम् ।
सूर्यां हिरण्मयीं लक्ष्मीं जातवेदो म आवह ॥१४॥

ārdrām yaḥ kariṇīm yaṣṭim suvarṇām hemamālinīm
sūryām hiraṇmayīm lakṣmīm jātavedo ma āvaha
||14||

O Jatavedas, please carry me to or bring to me the Divine Mother Lakshmi, who is wet, who embodies the power of action, who embodies the power of restraint, who is resplendent like gold and wears a necklace of gold.

O Jatavedas, please carry me to or bring to me the Divine Mother Lakshmi, who is the essence of the sun and as radiant as gold.

ārdrām, wet
yaḥ, the one who is
kariṇīm, embodiment of the power of action
yaṣṭim, staff symbolizing restraint; embodiment of the power of restraint
suvarṇām, resplendent like gold
hemamālinīm, the one who wears a necklace of gold
sūryām, the one who is the essence of, or the shakti of, the sun
hiraṇmayīm, the one who is the embodiment of gold; the one who is molten gold—living prosperity
lakṣmīm, the goddess of prosperity; the divinity endowed with all auspiciousness and goodness
jātavedas, O Omniscient Fire; O Most Sacred Fire presiding over rituals
ma, to me
āvaha, bring her from every direction in every respect

MANTRA 15

तां म आवह जातवेदो लक्ष्मीमनपगामिनीम् ।
यस्यां हिरण्यं प्रभूतं गावो दास्योऽश्वान् विन्देयं
पुरुषानहम् ॥१५॥

tām ma āvaha jātavedo lakṣmīmanapagāminīm
yasyām hiraṇyam prabhūtam gāvo dāsyo'śvān
vindeyam puruṣānaham ||15||

O Jatavedas, please carry me to or bring to me the Divine Mother Lakshmi, the one who having once come never goes away. In her may I obtain plentiful gold, cows, helpers, horses, and the company of humans.

tām, that
ma, to me
āvaha, bring her from every direction in every respect
jātavedas, O Omniscient Fire; O Most Sacred Fire presiding over rituals
lakṣmīm, the goddess of prosperity; the divinity endowed with all auspiciousness and goodness
anapagāminīm, the one who does not go away
yasyām, in the one in whom
hiraṇyam, gold
prabhūtam, plenty; abundant
gāvo, cows
dāsyaḥ, helpers; assistance; manpower
aśvān, horses
vindeyam, may I acquire
puruṣān, humans; human company
aham, I

MANTRA 16

यः शुचिः प्रयतो भूत्वा जुहुयादाज्यमन्वहम् ।
श्रियः पञ्चदशार्चं च श्रीकामः सततं जपेत् ॥१६॥

yaḥ śuciḥ prayato bhūtvā juhuyād ājyamanvaham
śriyaḥ pañcadaśarcam ca śrīkāmaḥ satatam japet ||16||

An aspirant desiring to receive the grace of the Divine Mother Sri should recite the fifteen mantras of Sri Sukta and should make the offering of ghee daily with purity and vigilance.

yaḥ, the one who
śuciḥ, clean
prayataḥ, vigilant
bhūtvā, upon becoming
juhuyād, should offer oblation
ājyam, of ghee
anvaham, every day
śriyaḥ, of Sri
pañcadaśarcam, the sukta consisting of fifteen mantras
ca, and
śrīkāmaḥ, desirous of Sri
satatam, without interruption
japet, should recite

APPENDIX B

The Sri Vidya Tradition

The tradition of Sri Vidya belongs to the unique school of Tantra—Shaktism—that integrates the experiences of Vedic sages and the philosophical ideas of Sankhya, Yoga, Mimamsa, and Vedanta. There are several subschools within Sri Vidya. We belong to the Samaya school, and more precisely, the Urdhva-Amnaya lineage. The first master of this lineage is the sage Kapila, who is also the first teacher of Sankhya philosophy. According to the *Sri Vidyarnava* by Vidyaranya Yati, there are seventy-one masters in the Urdhva-Amnaya lineage. They are as follows:

1. Kapila
2. Atri
3. Vashishtha
4. Sanaka
5. Sanandana
6. Sanatsujata
7. Bhrigu
8. Vamadeva
9. Narada
10. Gautama
11. Shunaka
12. Shakti
13. Markandeya
14. Kaushika
15. Parashara
16. Shuka
17. Angira
18. Kanva
19. Jabali
20. Bharadvaja
21. Vedavyasa
22. Ishana
23. Ramana
24. Kapardi
25. Bhudhara
26. Subhata
27. Jalaja
28. Bhutesha
29. Parama
30. Vijaya

31. Bharata
32. Padmesha
33. Subhaga
34. Vishuddha
35. Samara
36. Kaivalya
37. Ganeshvara
38. Supadya
39. Vibudha
40. Yoga (Patanjali)
41. Vijnana
42. Ananga
43. Vibhrama
44. Damodara
45. Chidabhasa
46. Chinmaya
47. Kaladhara
48. Vireshvara
49. Mandara
50. Tridasha
51. Sagara
52. Mrida
53. Harsha
54. Simha
55. Gauda
56. Vira
57. Aghora
58. Dhruva
59. Divakara
60. Chakradhara
61. Pramathesha
62. Chaturbhuja
63. Anandabhairava
64. Dhira
65. Gauda
66. Pavaka
67. Parasharya
68. Satyanidhi
69. Ramachandra
70. Govinda
71. Shankaracharya

This list was prepared more than a thousand years ago. Since that time, many more masters have enriched the tradition through their sadhana and their experiences. The names of some of the important masters passed on to me include:

Srinatha
Adinatha
Anadinatha
Anamayanatha
Anantanatha
Dattatreya
Parashurama
Vishnusharma
Pragalbhachaya
Vidyaranya Yati
Gorakhanatha
Minanatha
Dharamadasa (Madhvananda)
Atmarama
Abhayananda
Sadananda
Swami Rama

Note: In our tradition, we are told not to seek the physical identity of these masters or their dates. In recent years, for the sake of simplicity, we refer to our lineage as the Tradition of the Himalayan Masters or the Himalayan Tradition.

About the Author

Spiritual head and chairman of the Himalayan Institute, Pandit Rajmani Tigunait, PhD, is the successor of Swami Rama of the Himalayas. Lecturing and teaching worldwide for nearly 40 years, he is the author of 18 books, including his latest, *Vishoka Meditation: The Yoga of Inner Radiance,* as well as groundbreaking commentaries on the *Yoga Sutra* of Patanjali—*The Secret of the Yoga Sutra: Samadhi Pada* and *The Practice of the Yoga Sutra: Sadhana Pada.* He is a regular contributor to the Himalayan Institute's online Wisdom Library, the driving force of the Institute's global humanitarian projects, and the visionary behind the Institute's consecrated Sri Vidya Shrine in Honesdale, Pennsylvania.

Pandit Tigunait holds two doctorates: one in Sanskrit from the University of Allahabad in India, and another in Oriental studies from the University of Pennsylvania. Family tradition gave Pandit Tigunait access to a vast range of spiritual wisdom preserved in both the written and oral traditions. Before meeting his master, Pandit Tigunait studied Sanskrit, the language of the ancient scriptures of India, as well as the languages of the Buddhist, Jaina, and Zoroastrian traditions. In 1976, Swami Rama ordained Pandit Tigunait into the 5,000-year-old lineage of the Himalayan Masters.

HIMALAYAN INSTITUTE®

The main building of the Himalayan Institute headquarters near Honesdale, Pennsylvania

The Himalayan Institute

A leader in the field of yoga, meditation, spirituality, and holistic health, the Himalayan Institute is a nonprofit international organization dedicated to serving humanity through educational, spiritual, and humanitarian programs. The mission of the Himalayan Institute is to inspire, educate, and empower all those who seek to experience their full potential.

Founded in 1971 by Swami Rama of the Himalayas, the Himalayan Institute and its varied activities and programs exemplify the spiritual heritage of mankind that unites East and West, spirituality and science, ancient wisdom and modern technology.

Our international headquarters is located on a beautiful 400-acre campus in the rolling hills of the Pocono Mountains of northeastern Pennsylvania. Our spiritually vibrant community and peaceful setting provide the perfect atmosphere for seminars and retreats, residential programs, and holistic health services. Students from all over the world join us to attend diverse programs on subjects such as hatha yoga, meditation, stress reduction, ayurveda, and yoga and tantra philosophy.

In addition, the Himalayan Institute draws on roots in the yoga tradition to serve our members and community through the following programs, services, and products:

Mission Programs

The essence of the Himalayan Institute's teaching mission flows from the timeless message of the Himalayan Masters, and is echoed in our on-site mission programming. Their message is to first become aware of the reality within ourselves, and then to build a bridge between our inner and outer worlds.

Our mission programs express a rich body of experiential wisdom and are offered year-round. They include seminars, retreats, and professional certifications that bring you the best of an authentic yoga tradition, addressed to a modern audience. Join us on campus for our Mission Programs to find wisdom from the heart of the yoga tradition, guidance for authentic practice, and food for your soul.

Wisdom Library and Mission Membership

The Himalayan Institute online Wisdom Library curates the essential teachings of the living Himalayan Tradition. This offering is a unique counterpart to our in-person Mission Programs, empowering students by providing online learning resources to enrich their study and practice outside the classroom.

Our Wisdom Library features multimedia blog content, livestreams, podcasts, downloadable practice resources, digital courses, and an interactive Seeker's Forum. These teachings capture our Mission Faculty's decades of study, practice, and teaching experience, featuring new content as well as the timeless teachings of Swami Rama and Pandit Rajmani Tigunait.

We invite seekers and students of the Himalayan Tradition to become a Himalayan Institute Mission Member, which grants unlimited access to the Wisdom Library. Mission Membership offers a way for you to support our shared commitment to service, while deepening your study and practice in the living Himalayan Tradition.

Spiritual Excursions

Since 1972, the Himalayan Institute has been organizing pilgrimages for spiritual seekers from around the world. Our spiritual excursions follow the traditional pilgrimage routes where adepts of the Himalayas lived and practiced. For thousands of years, pilgrimage has been an essential part of yoga sadhana, offering spiritual seekers the opportunity to experience the transformative power of living shrines of the Himalayan Tradition.

Global Humanitarian Projects
The Himalayan Institute's humanitarian mission is yoga in action—offering spiritually grounded healing and transformation to the world. Our humanitarian projects serve impoverished communities in India, Mexico, and Cameroon through rural empowerment and environmental regeneration. By putting yoga philosophy into practice, our programs are empowering communities globally with the knowledge and tools needed for a lasting social transformation at the grassroots level.

Publications
The Himalayan Institute publishes over 60 titles on yoga, philosophy, spirituality, science, ayurveda, and holistic health. These include the best-selling books *Living with the Himalayan Masters* and *The Science of Breath*, by Swami Rama; *The Power of Mantra and the Mystery of Initiation, From Death to Birth, Tantra Unveiled,* and two commentaries on the *Yoga Sutra—The Secret of the Yoga Sutra: Samadhi Pada* and *The Practice of the Yoga Sutra: Sadhana Pada*—by Pandit Rajmani Tigunait, PhD; and the award-winning *Yoga: Mastering the Basics* by Sandra Anderson and Rolf Sovik, PsyD. These books are for everyone: the interested reader, the spiritual novice, and the experienced practitioner.

PureRejuv Wellness Center
For over 40 years, the PureRejuv Wellness Center has fulfilled part of the Institute's mission to promote healthy and sustainable lifestyles. PureRejuv combines Eastern philosophy and Western medicine in an integrated approach to holistic health—nurturing balance and healing at home and at work. We offer the opportunity to find healing and renewal through on-site wellness retreats and individual wellness services, including therapeutic massage and bodywork, yoga therapy, ayurveda, biofeedback, natural medicine, and one-on-one consultations with our integrative medical staff.

Total Health Products
The Himalayan Institute, the developer of the original Neti Pot, manufactures a health line specializing in traditional and modern ayurvedic supplements and body care. We are dedicated to holistic and natural living by providing products using non-GMO components, petroleum-free biodegrading plastics, and eco-friendly

packaging that has the least impact on the environment. Part of every purchase supports our Global Humanitarian projects, further developing and reinforcing our core mission of spirituality in action.

For further information about our programs, humanitarian projects, and products:

call: 800.822.4547
e-mail: info@HimalayanInstitute.org
write: The Himalayan Institute
952 Bethany Turnpike
Honesdale, PA 18431
or visit: HimalayanInstitute.org